COLLECTING

COINS

FRED SCHWAN

Alliance Publishers

ISBN 0-887110-02-X

Cover and interior design by Cynthia Dunne

Alliance Books are available at special discounts for bulk
purchases for sales and promotions, premiums, fund raising, or
educational use. Authors are available for public appearances
and interviews.
For details, contact:
Alliance Publishing, Inc.
P. O. Box 080377
Brooklyn, New York 11208-0002

Distributed to the trade by National Book Network, Inc.

10 8 6 4 2 1 3 5 7 9

ACKNOWLEDGMENTS

Even the smallest books require a team effort. One of the unstated facts in the following pages is that collecting is not only fun, but you also make great friends doing it! It is interesting that while collecting is a more or less solitary activity, it has many social aspects. It is easy to make friends with other collectors, because we share so many ideas, experiences, and frustrations too.

I have friends in many states and foreign countries as well. Some of them I see once or twice a year at a coin show or convention. Others I see frequently, and others I have never seen! They are all great friends.

Somewhere along the line I complained to Dorothy Harris, our editor, that I was not getting the hand holding that other authors of the Instant Expert series had attributed to her. Later I found that I was not ready for her guidance. When I finally got the manuscript developed enough for guidance, she had it for me. In guiding, nudging, and once or twice kicking me, Dorothy demonstrated to me the insight that she has for collecting. Others had told me that she was very wise in this way, but it was only when her wisdom could help the most that she gave it to me.

It was then that I realized that Dorothy is not only a publishing maven, but a collector. Yes, Dorothy Harris collects collectors! She looks for collectors the way we look for coins, stamps, and comics. When she finds one she wants, she pursues it and secures it so that she can take it out of her cabinet when it pleases her!

Cover art provided by the Smithsonian Institution (1933 $20 gold) and the American Numismatic Association. Text illustrations from the American Numismatic Association.

CONTENTS

Appendix

Epilogue
Index

NTRODUCTION

Pine tree shillings, pieces of eight, gold doubloons, eagles, double eagles, treasure! These words bring up youthful romantic memories. They are also a part of the fascinating world of coin collecting—specifically in the realm of collecting American coins.

Pine tree shillings were minted in Massachusetts in 1652.

President George Washington was interested in getting the federal coinage started. The Constitution gave the right of coinage to the federal government, but no coins had been produced by 1792. President Washington advanced $100 to buy the silver necessary to make a small start. Two thousand half dime coins were struck from that silver. From our twentieth century perspective, we can sense the frustration with bureaucracy that might have caused Washington to do what he did.

For more than 100 years the legend has circulated among coin collectors that George had turned Martha's sterling flatware over to the coiner to produce the coins. Although that story has been dis-

American coinage started with the 1792 half dime.

proved in favor of the one above, it has not died. Many collectors still tell it this way.

It is not possible to hold one of these 1792 coins in your hands without thinking of President Washington and the early years of the United States of America. This and a thousand other stories are part of the attraction of coin collecting.

We will talk about United States, colonial, and related issues here. While we do not address world coinage, many of the ideas and concepts as well as virtually all of the terminology used here apply to world coins as well as to United States coins.

WHAT IS AN INSTANT EXPERT?

American coinage is amazingly diverse, historically significant, popular to collect, and at the same time relatively easy to master. Various series of coins can be intricate, but compared to ancient coinages or those of European countries with many centuries of issues, American coinage is not too difficult to master. Perhaps this is one of the attractions of collecting United States coinage.

Believe it or not, you and your coin collecting friends are *numismatists* (pronounced noo mizz ma tists) and coin collecting is called *numismatics*. Numismatics encompasses more than coin collecting; paper money and medal collecting are included, as are a few other areas. It is a shame that we are stuck with such an unusual word, but we are. Get comfortable with using it.

To become an expert in one of the many fields of American coin collecting, you must first become something of a generalist; then you must select an area of specialization. Hence, the *Instant Expert.* Below you will find descriptions of most different types of American coins. You may choose to specialize in one of these, one of the other areas that we describe here, or some other area that you devise yourself.

THINK AND TALK LIKE AN EXPERT

CHAPTER 1

MARKET TRENDS

It is generally agreed that the coin market operates in *cycles*. In fact, many components of the coin market operate in cycles of their own. They are usually in agreement with the entire market, but not always. One theory has it that when prices go down as part of a cycle, they do not go nearly as low as the low of the preceding cycle and that when prices go up, they will generally go higher than previous highs. Coins on the upside of a cycle are said to be "hot," and of course those on the other end are called "cold." It is common for someone visiting a coin shop to ask what is hot. Commemorative coins and modern (1936 to present) proof set markets have definite cycles.

Without question, the long-term trend of coin prices has been up and will almost certainly continue that way. A major factor all but guaranteeing this trend is inflation. While the effects of inflation may be slow, they are very steady and are at work even during the dips and valleys of the coin market.

Not only does the market go up and down while following the inflationary pressure upward, but the many different coin series go up and down as well. Some go in phase, others out of phase, and still others independently, and certainly they seem to move unpredictably. Add to these factors the strong tie of part of the coin market to the price of gold and you will have a set of graphs that would make NASA proud!

Investing in coins is usually discussed early in any description of coin collecting. To many people, investing and collecting seem like the same thing; they are intertwined, to the extent that one generally must invest money to collect.

The key difference between collecting and investing is intent. A person who acquires an item because of the appeal of history and art is a collector; a person who buys the same item with the intent of making money is an investor. One can even read the IRS regulations and find the differences enumerated. Indeed, it can suit your purposes to follow those guidelines to help establish your status as one or the other.

You can make money in coins. Lots of money is made every year and every day of the year in coins by people other than full-time dealers (who also can make and lose money). However, my ironic advice to you, if you want to make money investing in coins, is to become a collector!

Collectors learn and appreciate what makes a particular coin interesting and desirable—or undesirable. In the final analysis, it is only the demand of collectors that makes the price of an item rise faster than inflation to create an actual profit for a seller. The first rule of most investment advisors is to diversify. Most collectors do that automatically because one of any particular coin is sufficient to satisfy the collecting desire.

Usually collectors who have studied their specialties and assembled quality collections of the respective issues have made money when selling their collections. This is certainly true when the passion was with the collector for twenty or more years, but money is frequently made in as little as five years.

Fads are related to cycles. It is not unusual for a type or category of coin to become very popular, and then suddenly lose popularity. If the popularity comes back, there is a cycle. Believe it or not there have been times when collectors sought entire rolls and even bags of a given coin! Specific errors and varieties often become hot upon discovery, and then get cold nearly as fast. Building sets of a specific type of coin by date and mint mark is a popular way to collect. When it first came into vogue about 100 years ago, many collectors considered it a fad! Before that time, sets consisted of one coin from each year with no regard to mint.

Rarity seems to be a simple concept. If few of something exist, they are rare and therefore must be valuable. In an absolute sense, the first idea of rarity is correct, but it is too strict for the numismatic market. Collectors (and dealers) like to buy things that are rare, but there are just not enough really rare things around for everyone to buy, so the term has taken on new meanings. First it is frequently used to describe coins that are at best scarce, particularly coins that are relatively scarce and in high demand. In a case like this, a relatively high price is created so everyone is comfortable calling the piece rare. After all, it has a high price.

An even more amazing development is the concept of *condition rarity*. This is a coin that may not be inherently rare but is rare in a particular condition. This concept had a noble beginning. All collectors prefer to have an attractive example of a given coin rather than a very worn example, and in the normal course of things, such nice examples are almost always scarcer than more worn pieces.

Now with professional grading and population reports, attempts are made to quantify the differences in rarity (as well as condition) between pieces with very little difference in actual condition. Assume the following statistics appear in the population report for coin X: MS-63 2000, MS-64 600, MS-65 60, MS-66 2. (In the numeral grading system coins are assigned numbers 1 through 70. The higher the number the better the condition.) We can safely say that coins in the MS-66 grade are more scarce than MS-64 and MS-63. We would have guessed this going in and it is unlikely that the relationship will change significantly when the next million coins have been graded. Does this make an MS-66 coin rare? Most important, how much is a 66 worth versus a 65 or a 64? These are questions best decided by a robust, mature market. Thus far the market has determined that there is a substantial difference in price between each of these grade levels. Often the price difference is exponential. The question that remains then concerns the maturity and robustness of the market. That is a matter of opinion.

What is it worth? This question in various forms is of constant interest to numismatists. In a theoretical sense, the answer is that the market will determine the price. As a practical matter, collectors looking to buy a coin want to know what price to pay. Price guides are published in book form, such as the ubiquitous "Redbook" *(Guidebook of United States Coins)*, as market reports in periodicals, and in newsletters.

You should purchase the latest edition Redbook and a periodical with a market report before you start buying coins. These reports are theoretical and are either estimates or out of date, but they are a good place to start. The best place to find the price that you will have to pay for a coin is to study the advertisements in one or several periodicals. You may be able to find a similar coin for a little less at a local coin shop or show, but you may also have to pay a little more. There is no hard and fast rule on this.

Newsletters also report values. By far the most common and successful newsletter of this type is the *Coin Dealer Newsletter*. It is known as "the Gray Sheet" or even just "the Sheet." The Sheet purports to list wholesale prices. In theory this sounds like the kind of information you would want to have before you start buying coins. As you probably guessed, there are several problems. The Sheet is a little bit expensive for beginners and it generally lists the higher value coins that beginners usually do not buy. Even beyond those considerations, the Sheet is not easy to use.

The Sheet lists wholesale prices on commonly traded United States coins. It offers bid and ask prices that are supposed to reflect the prices offered and asked by dealers in dealer-to-dealer transactions. This information nominally is correct, but wholesale and retail pricing is not nearly that easy in numismatics. Dealers routinely buy and sell above and below these levels based on inventory and capital needs as well as the specifics of the coin involved.

CONDITION

The condition of a coin is probably the most critical factor in determining its value. Therefore, grading of coins has been the subject of several books. It has also become a science—and a big business.

Extremely minor differences in the condition of a given coin can make a huge difference in the price of the piece. This situation created a new business, independent or third party grading services. These businesses employ staffs of experts who grade coins for a fee. The coins are then encapsulated with the grade report included as part of the plastic holder (called a slab). There are differences of opinion and even controversy among advanced collectors about commercial grading and slabs, but they provide a definite advantage for the beginner. If you plan to spend any serious money on coins before you have personal grading experience, buy coins that are slabbed.

Grading systems have evolved over the years and the standards are sometimes controversial. Several systems are still in use, but the dominate system is called the numerical grading system. Unfortunately, the system seems more intricate than it needs to be or is! In the numerical grading system, coins are assigned grades (numbers) 1 through 70. The higher the number, the better the condition.

The numbers 1 through 59 are used for the circulated grades. The most widely used grades (and numbers) are Good (G)-4, Very Good (VG)-8, Fine (F)-12 and 15, Very Fine (VF)-20 and 30, Extremely Fine (EF)-40 and 45, and About Uncirculated (AU)-55.

Coins that are uncirculated (without wear) are said to be in mint state and have Mint State (MS) numbers, MS-60 for example. However, because uncirculated coins may be of different quality, the numbers 60 through 70 are used to indicate the relative quality of the coin. Both MS-65 and MS-63 coins are uncirculated, but the MS-65 coin is much nicer than the other. MS-70 coins are said to be perfect. Some collectors contend that this is a theoretical grade because no perfect coins exist. In practice, a few, but very few coins, have been assigned the MS-70 grade by one of the major grading services.

MS-63 coins are sometimes called "select," MS-65 "gem," and MS-67 "superb," although the use of these adjectives is not uniform.

Most of the general public is vaguely aware of proof coins and proof sets. There is some argument about what constitutes a proof coin, but for practical purposes a proof coin is one that is struck on a specially prepared planchet (coin blank) with specially prepared dies. Usually they are struck more than once.

Today proof coins are prepared each year and sold to the public by the mint. Sets of proof versions of circulating coins are sold. Proof versions of commemorative coins are also sold either singly or as part of sets.

It seems strange at first, but the term proof describes a method of manufacture. It is *not* a condition. This is a difficult concept to digest even for some advanced collectors. Part of the reason is that most proof coins appear to be in better condition than most other, even uncirculated, coins. But it is quite possible for a proof coin to be found in less than uncirculated condition. Routine coins struck for circulation are called business strikes.

In the previous century, proof coins were sometimes forced into circulation because the owners needed the money. Even today, proof coins are put into circulation. Clerks who handle a large amount of change today report occasionally finding modern proof coinage. This might be because the rightful owner needs the money, but more often it is a way for a thief to get face value for stolen property.

Collectors have also been known to carry a proof coin as a souvenir. Of course the coin becomes worn in the process. I have personally carried modern proof coins as pocket pieces and had collectors comment that it *formerly* was a proof. Once a proof always a proof. However, a circulated proof is described as impaired.

The easiest way to demonstrate that a proof is always a proof is that some coins are produced only as proofs—no corresponding pieces are put into circulation. The most common example of this is modern proof sets that are struck at the San Francisco mint. There are no corresponding San Francisco circulating coins. No matter how worn it is, a 1994 San Francisco Kennedy half dollar is a proof.

As mentioned above, I have carried modern proof coins as pocket pieces. I carried a proof 1982 Washington commemorative half dollar until it was very worn. I had great fun asking the grading services to grade this coin. Of course they had never seen one so worn; it was always good for a laugh. The more interesting experiment was to ask them and other experts to determine whether the coin was a proof or circulation strike by looking at the reverse only (the telltale mint mark is on the obverse for this coin). It was remarkably easy to determine that it was a proof from the reverse only until the coin got down to grades of approximately Very Good (VG-8).

Proof coins are graded by essentially the same system as that described for *business strike* coinage above. The prefix P is used to differentiate proof grades from uncirculated business strike grades. As described above, proof coins can and are found in even the lower grades such as very good. For grading, circulated grade designations are used, so you will not find a P-45 coin on a price list.

A *raw* coin is one that has not been graded by one of the grading services. By inference it is one that has never been submitted, but this is not correct. It really means a coin that is not encapsulated by one of the services. It is possible to find raw coins with small bits of plastic showing that the coin had once been slabbed.

Fresh coins are those that have recently entered (usually reentered) the market. They have not been in inventory and passed over by other dealers and collectors. It is frequently assumed that raw coins are fresh and that fresh coins are not slabbed. Both of these assumptions are false.

A *slider* is a coin that has enough characteristics of a higher grade to be called that grade. It is desirable to purchase a slider at the price of the lower grade and very undesirable to buy it at the price of the higher grade.

Dealers and collectors frequently describe a coin as a 3, 4, or 5. They mean that it is MS-63, MS-64, or MS-65. The same system might be used for 1, 2, 6, and 7, but it is most often done for 3, 4, and 5, because the money involved is likely to be much more significant at these levels.

The following descriptions are very basic, but should help you as you start looking at coins or price lists.

Mint State-60 (MS-60): Basic or minimum mint state; a coin with numerous surface marks and abrasions as acquired in a mint or bank bag or at the mint itself. Grades from MS-61 to MS-70 (perfection) represent increasing quality.

About Uncirculated (AU-50, 53, 55, 58): With light wear, but with most of the luster in the fields remaining.

Extremely Fine (EF-40, EF-45): With more wear; with sharp design details in most areas, but with the luster gone.

Very Fine (VF-20, 25, 35): With more wear than the preceding and with some details of Miss Liberty's hair, eagle's feather, leaf veins, etc., gone, but with a generally bold appearance overall.

Fine (F-12, 15): With many details worn, but with all lettering, including the word LIBERTY, visible (with some exceptions).

Very Good (VG-8, 10): With more wear than the preceding. Only a few letters in LIBERTY readable.

Good (G-4, 6): Well worn, with LIBERTY gone, but with inscriptions such as UNITED STATES OF AMERICA, etc., minimally readable, sometimes with parts of the letters worn away.

About Good (AG-3): Worn nearly smooth. Nearly all features and inscriptions partially gone, but still identifiable.

Fair, Poor (Fair-2, Poor-1): The lowest possible grades. Identifiable as to denomination but varieties are identifiable only in a few cases.

Shortly after the grading services began business, they started publishing *population reports* of the number of coins that they had certified in any particular grade. For example, a report might show the "population" for Coin X as MS-63 2000, MS-64 600, MS-65 60, MS-66 2. Most collectors believe that these figures show the relative rarity between examples of Coin X in MS-63 and MS-65. Now that the services have graded millions of coins, this is a strong argument. There are several problems associated with this analysis. The biggest is that there has been a very strong trend to resubmit coins in the hope of getting a higher grade. There are cases reported of the same coin being submitted fifty times! This inflates the reports, because each time it is counted as if it were a new coin never before slabbed.

CONSERVATION AND RESTORATION GUIDELINES

Do not clean your coins. Even in the few exceptions to this rule, the cleaning should be left to experts if the coins are rare or valuable. Proof and uncirculated coins, especially silver dollars, are frequently dipped in a solution to remove surface material. When done carefully by an expert, this *may* be an acceptable practice, but you should not do it until you have thought it through and practiced on some low-value coins.

Fingerprints and other invisible materials on the surface of a coin can cause permanent damage when left over an extended period of time. Because of this, coins are sometimes dipped in trichlorotrifluoroethane before committing them to long-term storage. This is a harmless substance that neutralizes the surfaces of the coin to prevent damage from corrosion. This is a growing practice and is probably sound. Again, it is not a task for beginners.

You will want to store your coins in a safe, convenient way. There is no best way to store your collection and storage means have changed over the years. In the eighteenth and early nineteenth centuries collectors used wood cabinets to hold their collections. In the middle twentieth century, inexpensive albums helped fuel a boom in collecting. Other collectors used simple envelopes, then cardboard holders called "two by twos" (because they are 2 inches square) with cellophane windows for viewing the coins were developed. Custom plastic holders for expensive coins were very popular for a time. Capital Plastics of Massallion, Ohio, created a line of high-quality plastic holders for most American coins and could produce any holder needed. Plastic "flips" are the same size as a two by two and the common envelope. A flip is basically a double pocket envelope that allows you to put the coin in one side and a card with descriptive information in the other. All of the above supplies are still used to some extent, and of course they all have advantages and disadvantages, most of which boil down to personal preference.

However, there is one important aspect that is not a matter of preference. Preservation is the purpose of holders and some holders can damage your coins! The most dangerous is the plastic flip or page made with polyvinylchloride (PVC). This is the chemical that makes the item pleasantly pliable. Conventional envelopes also have chemicals that make them unsuitable for storing your coins.

Most two by twos and albums are safe for circulated and low-value uncirculated coins. Hard plastic flips are probably safe and Lucite holders are safe. Once you start getting serious about your collection, you should do some research on the way that is best for you. By that time you should know some other collectors or dealers. Ask them for advice.

Independent grading and subsequent encapsulation have had a big impact on the question of housing. Coins graded by the major services are sealed in plastic holders (slabs). These holders have been carefully designed to protect the coins, but since no coin has been in a slab for longer than ten years, their protective qualities are not yet fully proven. Plastic boxes have been designed to house slabs. Boxes of slabs fit nicely in safe deposit boxes, but they do not facilitate showing or even admiring your coins, and they take a lot of space.

WHERE TO BUY AND SELL

Coins may be obtained through the mail, at coin shows and shops, from other collectors, from auctions, and even from circulation. With the exception of the latter, you may also sell coins in these same places. Some people claim otherwise, but there is no single best place to buy or sell coins. The best place is the one that has the items you want at the price you want to pay (or receive).

Coin dealers are very important to the hobby and will probably be important to you as well. Coin dealers have shops in the major cities and many smaller ones, although there are not as many in small towns as there were in the 1960s. If you are lucky enough to have a local dealer, you should get to know him or her. If you have a local shop, be sure to visit it frequently. With luck, you will find a friendly atmosphere, but even if you do not, you can learn a great deal from the dealers and collectors you will meet there.

Mail order transactions account for the vast majority of coins bought and sold. This method offers many advantages to you. The biggest of these is that when you buy from a reputable dealer, you have a right of return. After receiving the coin, you can look it up in catalogs, read about it, consult with fellow collectors, and even take it to a coin show for consultation.

You generally start by obtaining the list of material for sale by a dealer. The easiest and fastest way is to read the advertisements in various publications. Some advertisements offer to send you lists upon request.

Study the lists. Compare prices, services, and guarantees. When you find something that you would like, try ordering it. If you find similar items offered by more than one dealer, order it from both and keep only the one that you like better! If there is a wide difference in the price, do not be surprised if there is also a wide difference in the quality of the material.

Obviously the **United States Mint** is the ultimate source of all of our coins. Unfortunately you cannot obtain all of the seventeenth and eighteenth century coins that you would like from the mint.

Collectors in those times did frequently get old coins from the mint. Today you can receive proof sets and other products from the mint. You should get on the mint mailing list by writing Box 7938, Philadelphia, PA 19162-0017.

Coin shows are held at least fifty weekends of the year. Except for the most remote areas, you should be able to find at least one show within a few hours drive to attend each year; for most collectors, many shows will be available.

Shows are the ideal place to see, hold, study, examine, and talk about coins. At the smaller shows you will probably see dealers from your local area. At larger shows you can meet dealers and other collectors from all over the country. Many of the shows are organized by local coin clubs. While you are there, inquire about when and where local clubs meet.

Coin World and *Numismatic News* publish lists of shows every week. They also have display advertising for the larger shows. Keep in mind that *Coin World's* list is paid advertising, whereas *Numismatic News* lists all (reported) shows, so it is recommended reading for finding shows.

Auctions provide another interesting and sometimes exciting way to study, learn, and perhaps buy coins. You can be a participant from the comfort of your home or on the auction floor. Auctions are held in conjunction with major coin shows and conventions, as well as independently in major cities.

The first thing that you should do is write to some of the major auction companies and ask for a copy of the catalog for the next sale. Companies generally charge a modest (but not cheap) price for these catalogs, but you can also find some that will send you a catalog or two for free. (If you even attempt to buy anything in their sales you probably will receive a few more for free) but that is getting ahead of ourselves.

In these catalogs you will find some of the very best numismatic photography and in many of them you will find excellent reading material. When the auction is over, the auction company publishes a list of prices realized (known as PRL). This is an additional research tool for you, but PRL are normally sent only to those who purchased the catalogs or who bought something in the sale.

Catalogs for past auctions can be very useful to beginners and advanced collectors alike. Many numismatists collect auction catalogs as avidly as coins and there are dealers who specialize in obsolete auction catalogs. You can frequently find catalogs of past but recent auctions at $1 or less at coin shops and shows.

The coins to be sold at auction are available for viewing before the sale. Viewing is a tremendous opportunity to study and hold many different coins including great rarities worth hundreds of thousands of dollars!

The viewing hours will be published in the catalog. Normally you must register as a bidder in order to view lots. You will want to register anyway, because this increases the chances that the auction company will send you additional catalogs and lists of prices realized. You will see that most people viewing lots also make notations in their catalogs. They are recording any characteristics that might influence their bids. They may also enter the highest bid that they are willing to make. This step is often done later, after the viewing, but you should always do it before the auction itself. Even if you do not intend to bid, you will probably find it interesting to estimate what you think a given item will sell for.

You will also want to attend the auction. At your first auction, you probably do not want to bid, but you should attend (frequently light refreshments are served at the sale). Study the hours so that you can attend a session that has coins of particular interest to you. Arrive early and take a seat in the back of the room. You will find a fairly intense group at the auction. Most people in the room are there to bid or are otherwise interested in the results. Most will write in their catalogs again. They enter notes for each lot or at least for lots in their areas of interest. You should do the same. At least enter the price realized. Many dealers and collectors take elaborate notes and might even use a personal code. You can develop your own system if you become a regular.

The atmosphere outside the auction room will be much more relaxed. There is a good chance that you will find people who have finished their business or who are waiting for "their" lots to be sold. In either case, there is a good chance that there will be something for you to learn.

There can be tactics and strategy in bidding in a sale, but in general if you want to bid on an item or two, you will not have any difficulty. Be sure to read the specific rules of the auction house, watch how the sale is conducted, and bid up to your limit on the items that you like.

You can also bid in a sale in absentia. You can submit a complicated list of bids or a single bid. The auction company will execute these bids for you without additional fees. This works just as though you were in attendance. Indeed, some people prefer to have the company execute the bids even though the bidder is present.

The above discussion relates to auctions by numismatic auction companies. You can also find coins in antique, estate, and other auctions. Here the situation is entirely different. Great coins have been purchased in such sales, but great mistakes have been made as well. We cannot give you much advice here, but we can offer the caution that great bargains are just as hard to find in this type of auction as in any other.

Private dealings are another way to buy, sell, and learn about coins. Many advanced collectors report that they enjoy the friendships that they have made in collecting even more than their collections! Collectors love to talk coins. Great finds, discoveries, and the great items that got away are always discussed when two or more collectors get together. Collectors are almost always looking for things to add to their collections, and they frequently have material for sale or trade. Once you have made the acquaintance of other collectors, you will probably want to buy some coins from them. Most advanced collectors will go out of their way to help new collectors.

However, somewhat ironically, the success of these dealings with your colleagues will depend more upon your knowledge than purchases made in less congenial ways. In mail order you have plenty of time to study before making a deal and have a return privilege. At auctions you have the opportunity to research and carefully deliberate about the price to pay before the auction, but you do not have a routine return privilege. In transactions with dealers in shops or at shows, you can study a coin, take time to study your notes, and consult with others before you buy. Frequently you will also have a return privilege when buying this way, but be sure to ask if you have any questions. When you buy from a fellow collector, you generally do not have any of these protections. On the other hand, you are less likely to need them.

Coin clubs are similar to coin shops and shows in that they offer you an opportunity to meet other collectors and learn about your hobby. As have local coin shops, coin clubs have dwindled in number since the 1960s and they vary in size and activity, but you should certainly try visiting your local club a few times. To find a local coin club, try calling a coin shop or collector friend, the American Numismatic Association, or Krause Publications.

You can still find coins for your collection **in circulation**! This seems hard to believe, but it is true. Most of these pieces are varieties or even errors, but they are interesting and possibly even valuable nonetheless. Dealer and author Scot Travers has been championing the idea that interesting and possibly even rare and valuable coins may be found in pocket change. In the October 1995

COINage, he listed ten examples. We will discuss three of these, but if this approach interests you, perhaps you should consult that article.

The first one is the 1995 double-die Lincoln cent. Although this is a minor variety, it is a wonderful coin because it captured the imagination of a large part of America in the spring of 1995. Front page stories in national publications proclaimed the rarity and value of this coin. The best part of it is that for a few weeks prices of $30 to $50 were paid to people who found these pieces in circulation. In my small home town, I am well known as an eccentric coin collector. Everywhere I went people asked me about this coin! I loved it. As all experienced collectors expected, the price of the coin fell as fast or faster than it rose, but it still exposed millions to our wonderful hobby.

Philadelphia mint 1982 Roosevelt dimes and 1989 Washington quarters can be found without a mint mark. This is in spite of the fact that the Philadelphia mint had started putting its mark on these coins in 1980. In the case of the dime, the mint mark was in fact mistakenly omitted. For the quarter, the area of the die bearing the mint mark was clogged with extraneous material so that the mint mark did not show. Although the cause was different in each case, the result was the same, an interesting variety that can still be found in circulation.

J. T. Stanton and Bill Fivaz have carried this idea to an extreme. They have gathered together information on these and *hundreds* of other coins that can be found in circulation or that can be found at coin shows at very low prices. The title of the book is a personal favorite of mine and it tells the whole story—*The Cherrypicker's Guide*.

Finally on this subject, "old timers" scoff at the idea of collecting from circulation, but virtually none of them have tried putting together from circulation a date and mint collection of Roosevelt dimes or Washington quarters from 1965 to date or Lincoln Memorial cents, introduced in 1959. These are not easy tasks and are certain to be fun.

As you head out to start your collection, remember one piece of numismatic wisdom: **Read the book before you buy the coin.** This slogan has been popular in numismatics for many years, but it was never more appropriate than today. The desktop computer has revolutionized numismatic publishing so that now there are one or more books available on most collecting specialties. The quality of the books varies, but you absolutely should learn from these authors.

You can buy a few numismatic books at major bookstores and virtually any book through the mail. Check the coin periodicals for advertisements of booksellers. However, the easiest place to start looking is at your local library. Look under "coins" and "numismatics" in the card catalog or computer. You are almost certain to find some things of interest. You are also likely to be disappointed, because something that you would like to read is missing. Remember this disappointment and after you have reviewed some more books from other sources, give the library a list of specific titles and authors that you recommend. Librarians are always happy to receive suggestions from local patrons, and your assistance might help another collector.

To make things even easier, books exist on most series of coins that provide detailed information of the type that collectors of only a generation ago had to study for years—or decades—to learn. These books certainly cannot teach you everything about any particular series of coins, but they can teach you enough to walk and talk like an expert on the series in question.

This proliferation of books has been brought about by two factors. The first is the trend toward specialization that came into vogue in the 1970s and has become even stronger. One reason for the rise in specialization was the dramatic increase in prices from the 1950s through the 1990s. It became increasingly difficult for a collector to afford to be a generalist. The other factor was new technology in the publishing industry that allowed the publication of specialized short-run books.

The American Numismatic Association maintains the world's largest circulating library. The cost of membership can easily be recovered by the free use of books from the library. The librarian will send you most books or catalogs that you want in exchange for paying the postage and insurance both ways.

THE LANGUAGE OF COLLECTING

Juice is the commission charged to the *buyer* by most auction firms. Buyers' fees are a relatively new phenomenon on the American numismatic auction scene. After the first major firm introduced it in the 1970s as a way to reduce the traditional commission charged to the seller, it only took a few years before all of the major firms adopted it. When looking at a coin in a dealer's inventory at a coin show, you might say something like, "I saw a similar coin in a recent auction, but I just hate paying the juice."

A *rip* is a great bargain. When a person buys such a coin, he or she is said to have ripped the seller. This is slightly different from buying a sleeper. The implication is that the person ripped did not appreciate the value of the item even though it was probably correctly identified.

A rip is also a *score* and a deal where a dealer made a lot of money is a *homer*.

The term *bottom feeder* is usually used derisively to describe a collector or dealer who only buys at rock bottom prices. It is not necessarily bad to be a bottom feeder or to have a reputation as a bottom feeder. If you are looking to purchase a wide variety of items at the lowest possible prices, you are a bottom feeder and it might be appropriate to call yourself one. On the other hand if you are looking for top-quality or especially rare items, you do not want to appear to be a bottom feeder, because you will probably not be offered these items.

A *sleeper* is an underappreciated item. It may be an entire series of coins that is not popular with collectors at a particular time, or a particular issue of a given series that is more difficult to obtain than most collectors realize. Almost by definition the status of an item as a sleeper is an opinion by the numismatist in question.

It is very popular to hunt thorough a dealer's inventory looking for items that are not fully attributed as to variety, not correctly graded, or otherwise are underpriced. A *cherry* is different from a sleeper even though in both cases the buyer might be using superior knowledge about the item. Sleepers are generally correctly identified and priced but the buyer believes that the entire market is incorrect. A cherry is an item that the seller does not fully appreciate. The term cherry is not often used in this context but the term *cherry picking* is commonly used.

COIN TERMINOLOGY

The sides of a coin have funny names, but it is very important that you use the accepted terminology. You will be instantly branded as a rookie if you call the *obverse* of the coin the front, heads, or something else. These terms adequately define obverse for you, but do not use them. The other side is the *reverse*. Connecting the obverse and the reverse is the *edge*. The raised parts at the edges of the edge are the *rims*.

Toning is the sometimes colorful oxidation of the surface of a coin. Collectors will pay more for coins with attractive toning, but they cannot decide what attractive is. Because attractive toning can command a premium, people have artificially toned coins or, even worse, cleaned and then artificially toned them. Anthony Swiatek has experimented with ways to artificially produce toning and reported the results in his newsletter *The Swiatek Numismatic Report.*

Swiatek reports the following methods of applying artificial toning (none recommended): a weak concentration of a sulfur solution can cause a gold to golden brown tone; a sulfur shampoo can create green, yellow, and brown colors if left on the coin for a day or longer; and—are you ready for this—a coin baked inside an Idaho potato covered with corn oil and wrapped in foil can take on a purple-blue to orange color!

$\mathscr{H}$ISTORY
OF AMERICAN
COINS

MINTS AND MINT MARKS

Coins are manufactured, or struck, at mints. Note that mints do not print paper money, although you will frequently find the terminology used this way in the general media. However, there has been some quibbling about the mint terminology over the years. Various facilities where coins were minted in the United States have been officially called assay offices or bullion depositories even though coins were minted there.

The Philadelphia mint was founded in 1793 and has minted coins continuously since then. Branch mints have been established to assist in the manufacturing of coins. The westward expansion and economic development of the nation can be traced by the establishment of these branch mints in the nineteenth century. Several were directly linked to silver and gold strikes.

As most people are aware, mint marks are applied to most coins to identify the mint of origin, although there have been exceptions in

27

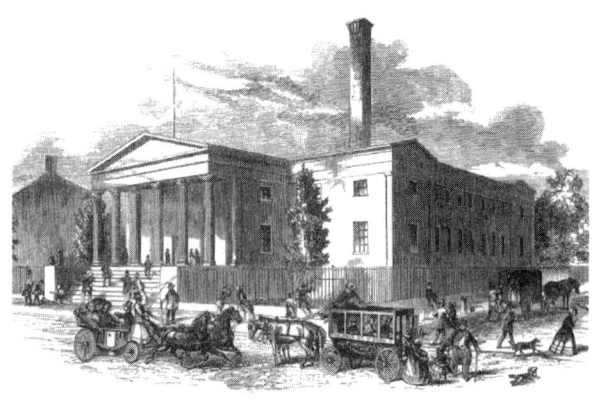

The United States mint building in Philadelphia 1833–1901. This building is known as the second mint building. The profile of the first mint building is at left.

recent years. This is an ancient tradition in minting that has little practical application today, but the mint marks are of great interest to collectors.

The various United States mints are listed below with essential data and some commentary.

The Philadelphia mint (1793 to present) did not use a mint mark until 1942. Philadelphia coins were (and are) described by collectors as "plain" because they do not have a mint mark. A collector says, "I am looking for a 1921 plain dime," meaning a 1921 Philadelphia mint product as opposed to "…21-D," meaning a Denver product.

Philadelphia mint mark above Monticellio dome on wartime coin.

In 1942, the composition of the 5¢ coin was changed to a silver alloy because nickel was a strategic metal. When this was done, the size and position of the mint marks were changed and a P mint mark was introduced for Philadelphia products. That was the first instance of the use of a mint mark by the Philadelphia mint. In 1979 the P was reintroduced and has appeared on coinage since then except for the Lincoln cent, which maintained the tradition of having no mint mark for Philadelphia.

Mints were established in Charlotte, North Carolina (C), and Dahlonega, Georgia (D), in 1838 to mint gold that was mined locally. The mints operated until 1861. Their coinage is generally rare and expensive.

The New Orleans (O) mint was also established in 1838. However, it lasted until 1909 and produced large quantities of coins, many of which are very inexpensive in circulated condition.

The Carson City, Nevada (CC), mint was established in 1870. Although it closed after only a few years of operations (in 1893), it too had significant production so that some of its coins can be acquired inexpensively today. In addition, the federal treasury sold large quantities of silver dollars in the 1960s that were left from the Carson City years, so it is even possible to obtain uncirculated examples for modest prices.

The Denver (D) mint started in 1906 with silver and gold coinage. It is a major facility today.

The San Francisco (S) mint has been the longest lived branch mint. It was established in 1854 and

The D and S mint mark appear on the obverse of the Walking Liberty half dollar below the date in 1916 and 1917.

San Francisco was the first branch mint to produce cents. Its mint mark appears below the wreath on the reverse.

operates today even though it was closed from 1956 to 1966. Among other distinctions, the San Francisco mint was the first branch mint to strike one cent coins when it produced Indian cents in 1908.

The West Point (W) mint first came into prominence when its mint mark appeared on the 1984 Olympic commemorative coins. The W has not appeared on any circulating coinage, but 1985 cents were struck at West Point without a mint mark.

The following brief descriptions will allow you to find the mint marks on unfamiliar coins:

Half cents, large cents, flying eagle cents—all minted in Philadelphia without mint mark.

Indian cents (1908 and 1909 only, S mint mark only)—under the wreath on the reverse.

Lincoln cents—under the date.

Two cents, three cents (copper-nickel)—all minted in Philadelphia without mint mark.

Three cents (silver)—all minted in Philadelphia without mint mark except for the 1851 which has the New Orleans "O" to the right on the reverse.

Shield nickels—all minted in Philadelphia without mint mark.

Liberty Head nickels—all minted in Philadelphia without mint mark except for 1912 which has a "D" or "S" to the left of CENTS on the reverse.

Jefferson nickels 1938–1941 and 1946–1964—on the reverse at the right of the building.

Jefferson nickels 1942–1945—above the dome on the reverse (including the first use of the "P" for Philadelphia).

Half dimes—on the reverse side either within or below the wreath.

Bust dimes, quarters, half dollars, and dollars—all minted in Philadelphia without mint mark.

Seated dimes—on the reverse below the wreath.

Winged Liberty head dimes—on the reverse to the left of the base of the faces.

Roosevelt dimes 1948–1964—on the reverse at the left bottom of the torch. From 1968 on the obverse above the date.

Twenty cents—reverse under the eagle.

Seated quarters—on the reverse below the wreath.

Liberty Head (Barber) quarters and half dollars—on the reverse below the eagle's tail feathers.

Standing Liberty quarters—on obverse to the left of the date.

Washington quarters—1932–1964 on the reverse under the eagle. From 1968 on the obverse to the right of Washington.

Bust half dollars (1838 and 1839 only)—"O" above the date.

Seated and Liberty head (Barber) half dollars—on the reverse below the eagle.

Walking Liberty half dollars—1916 below the date, 1918 and later on the reverse at lower left. For 1917 both locations were used.

Franklin half dollar—on the reverse above the bell beam.

Kennedy half dollar—1964 on the reverse at left near claw and laurel. From 1968 on obverse under the Kennedy portrait.

Bust dollars, seated dollars—all minted in Philadelphia without mint mark.

Seated and Morgan dollars—on the reverse below the wreath.

Peace dollars—on the reverse at the lower tip of the eagle's wing.

Eisenhower dollar—on the obverse above the date.

Anthony dollar—on the obverse to the left of the bust.

Trade dollars—on the reverse under the eagle.

Gold dollars—on the reverse under the wreath.

Quarter eagles—1838 and 1839 over the date; other dates before 1907, on the reverse under the eagle. Indian type on the reverse at the lower left.

Three dollars—on the reverse under the wreath.

Half eagles—1838 and 1839 over the date; other dates before 1907, on the reverse under the eagle. Indian type on the reverse at the lower left.

Eagles—on the reverse under the eagle; after 1907 at the left of the denomination.

Double eagles—on the reverse under the eagle; Saint-Gaudens type on the obverse above the date.

American Eagle gold bullion coins—on the proof version only on the obverse between second and third rays at right below the date.

American Eagle silver bullion coins—on the proof version only on the reverse to the left of the eagle's tail.

COIN TYPES

United States coinage began in 1792 with the minting of a half dime. Since that prototype was produced, untold billions of coins have been produced at American mints. The history, art, economics, and sheer fascination represented by these coins is unmatched by any country during these two centuries.

For ease of collecting, coins are informally classified into groups called types. A type is a major design. For example, the lowly Lincoln cent is a coin type, as is the Jefferson nickel. Because it is an informal system, there are some differences in the names that the different types are called. In addition, a type like Lincoln cents can include subtypes and/or varieties. The differences between a type and a variety are also not firm.

In 1909 the first Lincoln cent was produced. It had the initials of the designer somewhat prominently placed at the bottom of the reverse. Later in the year the initials were removed altogether. In 1959 the Lincoln Memorial replaced the wheat ear design for the reverse of the Lincoln cent. To some collectors all of these changes created new types. To others removal and later (1914) restoration of the initials created varieties, but the complete change of the reverse created a new type.

There is no perfect answer as to what is a type and what is a variety, but it is certain that type collecting is a very popular way to approach American coinage. In type collecting, you attempt to collect only one (or perhaps two) of each type within a larger area of interest. It is popular to build a twentieth century type set for example. A nineteenth century type set is much more challenging. A collection might be further limited as a bronze and nickel twentieth century type set, or a bronze, nickel, and silver set.

Of course you are familiar with all of the current types, but you are probably not so familiar with the obsolete series. Until the twentieth century, one design was used for all or most of the silver coins in circulation. There were some varieties and differences in dates of change from one type to another,

bust
(1790s)

Liberty seated
(1839)

Barber
(1892)

transition
(1916)

portrait
(1930s–40s)

but the designs were substantially the same for 10¢, 25¢, and 50¢ denominations, and only slightly less so for $1 coins.

Furthermore, if we look at the discontinuation of this system in 1916, we find that although the next designs were not even close to being the same, they were at least similar in theme and, more important for our purposes here, they were transitional issues until the introduction of the portrait coins. From this simplistic view the entire history of our silver coinage can be described as shown at left:

A type set certainly demonstrates the greatest amount of art, history, and economics in the fewest number of coins. The following abbreviated list of types outlines the entire history of United States coinage and provides a convenient outline for a discussion of collecting possibilities. You might well decide to specialize in one of the types listed below. All of them are worthy of such attention, but I have included some personal opinions about the desirability of the various series for that purpose. The list is repeated at the end of the book with space for your convenience.

Half Cents and Large Cents:
Half cents 1793–1857. Many non-collectors are surprised that we had this denomination. You can easily imagine that a half cent coin had a fair purchasing power in the 1790s. Its size alone indicates

Yes, we had a half cent coin 1793–1857! They are historic and popular with collectors.

1793 cents and half cents are among our most historic coins.

the relative value of a half cent. The half cent was eliminated in conjunction with the reduction in the size of the cent in 1857.

The designs of the half cents and large cents were substantially the same: liberty cap, draped bust, classic head, and coronet types. The large cent was introduced first and had an additional flowing hair type that appeared only in 1793, which included several varieties. All of the 1793 coinage is at least moderately rare and very much in demand as the first year of our copper coinage so it is quite expensive. Other dates in the 1700s are more reasonable, but still at least somewhat expensive. It is possible, however, to get a very well worn example for less than $100, which is not all that much for such a historic piece.

However, half and large cents present great opportunities for specialization. You can obtain

The large cent 1793–1857 is a classic coin. It has always been popular with collectors.

many different pieces from the very early 1800s through 1857 at modest prices, and have a lifetime of fun doing it. Interesting varieties abound and many of them have not been properly identified and wait to be cherrypicked from dealer stocks.

Small Cents:

Cents of the current size (diameter) were introduced in 1857 and have been produced every year since. A trial piece (pattern) was produced in 1856 with a mintage of about 1,500. This mintage is very high for such a piece so it is often considered the first year of issue. The design was a beautiful flying eagle, but it lasted only two years. If you want to have a complete collection of a United States type coin, this may be the easiest to finish with only two years required. Although the series is somewhat popular with collectors, it has seldom been hot, and could be a very good place for you to start an interesting collection.

The flying eagle design was only used for three years 1856-1858.

The flying eagle cent was replaced in 1859 by the Indian head cent, a long-lived design popular with the public and collectors alike. In 1908 the San Francisco mint became the first branch mint to strike cents. Its mint mark appears on Indian cents of 1908 and 1909. Even though Indian cents have been very popular with collectors for many years, if you are interested in collecting nice circulated

The Indian cent is a beautiful and popular coin.

coins, you can have a lot of fun building a set for not too much money.

The Indian head cent is responsible for starting many of today's senior numismatists in collecting. A few of these coins could be found in circulation in the 1950s and they were commonly found in the 1940s, so many collectors started by finding these strange coins in change. Even those who did not actually find any Indian heads in circulation had parents and friends who had saved a few from those years. Even today, it is not unusual for a beginning collector to find a relative who has a few Indians to share.

The Lincoln cent was the first coin to portray an actual person when it was introduced in 1909. The first design included the initials of the designer, Victor David Brenner (V. D. B.) fairly prominently on the reverse. There was some objection and the ini-

Lincoln was the first president portrayed on a coin.

tials were removed, creating two varieties. Since the coin was manufactured in Philadelphia and San Francisco in both varieties, there are actually four Lincoln cents to collect for 1909. If you like, you can add the San Francisco and Philadelphia Indian cents to make a really interesting collection of 1909 cents.

The San Francisco product with initials had a mintage of only about half a million. This low mintage combined with extreme popularity has always made this a relatively high-priced coin.

This is in spite of the "first year phenomenon." It may seem a little surprising, but generally the very first year of issue for a given coin is one of the most common. The reason for this is that when a new coin is introduced, it catches the eye of the general population and disproportionate numbers are saved by these curiosity seekers. An uncertain number of rolls of 1909-S VDB cents was saved in this way, much to the delight of future generations.

With its very long history (the longest of any United States coin), the Lincoln cent has a lot to offer any collector. Veteran collectors would be surprised at how challenging it is to build a Lincoln Memorial cent set from circulation. These collectors have forgotten the thrill of the search that got many of them started!

You can also assemble a year set 1909 to the present without too much difficulty or expense unless you want examples in top condition. Remember, collecting by date was the preferred method until date and mint collecting caught on in the twentieth century. Of course, if you want to collect a "complete set," you will have a challenging and interesting task—and expensive if you want mint state coins.

By the way, our smallest denomination coin is not a "penny," it is a "one cent piece" or just a "cent." The practice of calling it a penny began when the first copper coins were introduced. The English had a large copper coin that was properly called a penny. Americans immediately started using penny to describe large cents. Of course this terminology is still used by the general public. You will even hear collectors use it occasionally. They usually use it in a slightly humorous way, as in "I am nothing but a penny collector." The blue folders still used by some collectors to house their collections are sometimes called penny boards (even when referring to albums for other denominations).

For many years the small cent was the most collected coin. It may still be; it certainly is a popular coin for collectors. The emphasis in recent years has been away from the cent, however, so it may be a place for you to specialize!

Two and Three Cents:

Two cent pieces, a more or less ill-fated experiment, were issued for only ten years (1864–1873) and they have languished in collecting obscurity ever since. This is probably because most collectors are looking for a wider challenge, but these historic coins would make an excellent place for you to start collecting. "In God We Trust" appeared first on this coin. If you like it you will probably find enough varieties and diversity to keep you going for a while.

The motto "In God We Trust" was introduced with the 2 cent piece.

Two decidedly different three cent coins were issued in the second half of the 1800s. Three cent silver coins were minted 1851–1873. They have the interesting nickname "trime." These are the smallest American silver coins ever to circulate. The coins are just over .5 inch in diameter and the

The nickel 3 cent coin may be the most neglected in American numismatics.

weight was reduced in 1854 to approximately .02 oz. They are very thin and feel like nothing in your hand. Trimes were supplemented, then replaced, by nickel three cent coins 1865-1889.

The nickel 3¢ coins might well be the least studied American minor coin. Relatively few varieties have been identified, but it is still a fascinating coin series. Overall the mintages were very low. Some years had only proof issues and some years even had more proofs than business strikes. All of this makes for good opportunities for your specialization.

Many of the comments regarding collecting the 2¢ pieces above apply to the 3¢ coins. Obviously the denomination provides more variety with more years to consider. One interesting twist is that the 1851 trime was minted in Philadelphia as would be expected for that era. It was also minted in New Orleans, making it the smallest denomination produced at a branch mint until the 1908 cent was minted in San Francisco.

Half Dimes:

The 5¢ denomination was introduced in 1794 along with other denominations above 1¢. The twist is that the coin was silver and called a half dime rather than a nickel! In current catalogs the 5¢ nickel coins are listed first followed by the half dimes. This is so that the half dimes will be listed in

The 1792 half dime is an ultimate example of "history in your hands."

association with the dimes that follow. This is a convenient method. However, chronologically it is incorrect because the half dimes were issued first.

As stated in the introduction, the half dime was introduced by President Washington in 1792. Arguably that was the first coin of the United States of America. Actually that 1792 piece was a pattern (trial). Half dimes for general circulation were introduced in 1794 along with the other silver coinage. Therefore its designs follow the pattern of silver coinage described above, but it stopped with the Liberty seated design. Half dimes are tiny, but they have their own fascination. Many varieties have been recognized and are collected. In their time half dimes did circulate heavily. It is very common to find well worn pieces, so it is possible to build a date or date and mint set at modest cost although it would take many years to complete or even approach completeness.

In the 1970s a collector bought a worn 1870 San Francisco half dime from a dealer. The price was modest, actually cheap by any standard. The collector paid the going rate for any common Liberty seated half dime in that condition, $15 perhaps. It turned out that that was the only 1870-S half dime that had ever been found. It was not in any museum or collection!

The coin was sold to a Chicago coin firm for an undisclosed price. That firm subsequently sold it to a dealer from Michigan in an interesting transaction. The owner wanted to sell and the prospective buyer wanted to buy, but at what price. They agreed that the price would be $25,000 higher than the price realized on an 1804 silver dollar that was going to appear in an auction. The dollar sold for about $400,000 so the price paid was about $425,000. In 1986 the Michigan dealer decided to sell the 1870-S half dime. It sold at auction for $253,000. Of course that was a tremendous loss for that seller, but still not bad for a coin that was plucked from common stock ten years before!

Nickels:

Five cent nickel pieces, or nickels, were introduced in 1866 and have been used continuously ever since, but only four designs have been created. There are plenty of possibilities for collectors here. In fact every design type represents an opportunity. The first two types, shield 1866–1883 and Liberty head 1883–1912, have only very modest followings. This spells opportunity! You might want to start by putting together date sets of very low grade pieces for correspondingly low prices. As you do this you can have some fun and learn a lot about both series. Then you can decide if you want to get more serious and move into higher grades.

When the Liberty head nickel was introduced in 1883, it did not have the word "cents" as part of the design. It had a large roman numeral on the reverse that was supposed to suffice. The con artists of the

The shield design was the first for a nickel 5 cent coin.

day quickly seized an opportunity, because the $5 gold piece was approximately the same size as the nickel. They gold-plated the 5¢ coins and passed them as $5 gold pieces! When played at its best, the customer (con artist) presented merchandise worth less than 5¢ and offered the plated coin in payment. He then left with the merchandise and the change—nearly $5!

The mint realized quickly the effect of its mistake and altered the design to include the word "cents" as part of the reverse design, creating two different varieties of the coin. Today these plated coins are known as "racketeer nickels."

A coin dealership recently plated some of the 1883 coins and sells them as re-creations of the racketeer nickel. This enterprise is made possible by the first year phenomenon because the 1883 nickel "without cents" is a very common coin. It is much more common than its counterpart "with cents." This is in spite of the fact that the mintage of the "with cents" coin is much greater (16 versus 5 million).

The 1913 Liberty head nickel is one of the most famous coins in the world. It has been paraded before the general public in television murder mysteries and many other ways. There are only five of these pieces. Although they were made at the Philadelphia mint, they were not legitimate mint products, but their true and complete pedigree is unclear. However, once they left the mint, they had a profound effect on the hobby. The first few owners had all five coins. One of these owners was B. Max Mehl, who was the most prominent dealer of the period 1930–45. Mehl advertised heavily to buy coins; he advertised in print and on the radio and sold lists of coins he would buy. Searching pocket change for valuable coins became a fad because of Mehl. The showpiece of his advertising was the 1913 Liberty nickel. He offered to pay what seemed to be a huge price for a coin that the public thought should be easy to find. The psychology was not much different from state lotteries in the 1990s!

Mehl made money buying and selling coins, but he made a lot of money selling lists!

The final chapter has not been written on the 1913 Liberty nickel. Aubrey Bebee made national news when he paid $20,000 for one of the pieces in the 1950s. Later he carried it around in his pocket (in a holder) to show his collecting friends. Eventually he donated his 1913 nickel to the museum of the American Numismatic Association, where it can be seen today. In the 1990s there is some doubt about the current disposition of the other pieces. There have even been claims that one of the five was lost in an automobile accident.

The last two design types, Indian head or buffalo 1913–1938 and Jefferson 1938–present, are of course much better known to the general public and are indeed more popular with collectors than the first two types. Everyone loves the buffalo nickel. Usually that would mean that we must pay high prices for them. Fortunately that is not completely true in this case. Not only can you work on a worn date set for very low prices, but you can also purchase some very nice uncirculated pieces for low prices! Of course you cannot get the key dates in uncirculated condition at the same low prices.

I think that the most opportunities might exist in the Jefferson type. First, you may start from your pocket change and find more different dates and mints than you think. Of course you can supple-

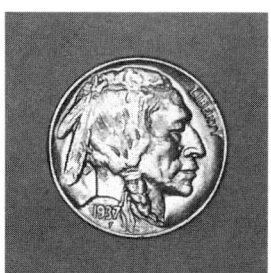 

The Indian head or buffalo nickel has always been a very popular design.

The Jefferson 5 cent coin was made of silver during World War II.

ment those finds by searching accumulations that your friends and neighbors might have. Actually, you can buy a complete uncirculated set for not very much money. However, these ideas gloss over the opportunities.

There are many interesting things about the Jefferson nickel. The most obvious is that during the war years 1942–45 it was not even made of nickel! Its composition was changed to a silver alloy in order to conserve nickel. That is interesting enough in itself, but consider that tremendous quantities of these "warnicks" were melted in the silver booms of the 1960s and 1980s and you can see a complex situation developing.

The 1950 Denver nickel had a mintage of about 2.5 million (very low by current standards). Everyone knew this and the coin was hoarded in huge quantities. Collecting—or rather buying and hoarding—1950-D Jeffersons became a rage. Rolls and bags and even truckloads of the coins were sold. The price went up fast. When the insanity stopped, the price came down equally fast. You can buy a nice uncirculated example today for much less than you could in 1955 and it is difficult to find a circulated example.

You could have fun specializing in Jefferson nickels!

Dimes:

Dimes were not introduced until 1796. They followed the design scheme for silver coinage. The early types have the normal distribution of interesting varieties and you can find many worn pieces for low prices or spend a fortune building a date and mint collection.

Another of the great rarities of American numismatics is included in the Liberty head (Barber) dimes. In 1894 only twenty-four pieces were minted in San Francisco. The exact reason for this mintage is debated, but it remains unambiguously one of the great rarities. To make matters more interesting, all twenty-four pieces have not been accounted for! In the 1990s the Professional Numismatists Guild held a nationwide treasure hunt to find the missing 1894-S dimes and other rarities. Remarkably, one of the dimes was found! It was not one that had been "missing" since 1894, but it had not been accounted for by collectors in about fifty years.

The transition series for this denomination is a wonderful design officially called the winged Liberty head, but more commonly called Mercury dimes by collectors. There are only a few varieties, but the series is still interesting. Perhaps this is because it had moderately low mintages during the 1920s and 1930s then served during World War II.

The Mercury dime is a beautiful coin. In 1942 some dies were created from those left over from 1941. This interesting variety was created.

The Roosevelt dime was introduced in 1948 shortly after the president's death (in 1945).

A famous variety of the 1942 date was created when dies from 1941 were altered to 1942 dates (this type variety is called an overdate).

The Roosevelt dime is one of the great yawns in numismatics. There is very little to attract a collector except to try to find the 1965 to the present issues in circulation. You might have fun doing that. You can also purchase a complete, uncirculated date/mint set for a very modest amount. Normally, when a series is not popular with collectors, I recommend that it represents an opportunity. In this case I cannot see any likelihood that collectors will give any great attention to this issue for a good long time.

In 1875 a 20¢ denomination was added to the complement of circulating coinage. It was met with less than enthusiastic response by the public and effectively discontinued in 1876. Although addi-

The 20 cent denomination is a curiosity today.

tional coins were struck in 1877 and 1878, they were proofs for collectors. The Carson City mint produced a substantial quantity of this coin in 1875, so that issue is an ideal candidate for a type set fulfilling the need for a 20¢ piece and a coin from Carson City. In 1876 Carson City minted an additional 10,000 pieces, but because of the lack of popularity with the public, most of these coins were melted, creating another great rarity.

Collectors do not seem to care much for this coin. Probably this is because there are so few coins to collect. While this is true it also makes it relatively easy for you to study all there is to find about this series. I like these coins.

Quarters:

Quarters were introduced in 1796 with the dime and have been used continuously since then. The early types—draped bust (1796–1807), capped bust (1815–1818), Liberty seated (1838-1891), and Barber or Liberty head (1892–1916)—abound with varieties, low mintages, and scarce issues. However, if you will settle for well-worn examples, you can still obtain many historic and interesting coins at low prices. Again, going after low-value coins can teach you a lot so that if you move up to "nicer" coins, you will be loaded with knowledge.

The standing Liberty quarter was introduced in 1916 to very bad reviews. Hermon MacNeil's design was very different from anything before or

The standing Liberty coin was a radical design when introduced in 1916.

since, but the poor reception had to do with morals, not art. Miss Liberty was striding forward with a breast exposed! This was too much for the public, or at least a vocal minority. MacNeil was ordered to "fix" his design and he responded by covering Liberty's chest with chain mail.

The entire series is remarkable in many ways. Although uncirculated examples are very beautiful, the coin did not wear well. Unlike quarters of the earlier types, standing Liberty quarters in the lower grades are not attractive and the dates are usually illegible or nearly so.

Nonetheless, these coins are popular with collectors. Why is this? It is difficult to say for sure, but it has not always been this way. Harry Foreman has been a well-known dealer for many years. In the 1960s he wrote one of the first books on investing in United States coins. He gave advice that is still good today and which has been implied above: stay away from fad and popular coins. He went on to describe each coin series with respect to its prospect for investment. I remember very well what he had to say about these quarters because they were among my favorite coins (I was collecting them from circulation at the time). He described the standing Liberty quarter as being unpopular and there was no likelihood that the situation would change.

One of the real disappointments of the standing Liberty quarter series is that no proof examples were officially struck. This is a particular shame in this case because this coin is probably the most uniformly poorly struck type of all American coins. I would love to own a proof of a common date standing Liberty quarter; unfortunately, there just are not any.

No quarters were struck in 1931. In 1932 the Washington quarter was issued as a commemorative. No quarters were struck again in 1933 (not many coins of *any* denomination were struck in 1933). The Washington design was then retained when coinage of the denomination was resumed in 1934.

The Washington quarter was intended to be a commemorative when it was introduced in 1932.

In many ways, I should be as pessimistic about the Washington quarter as I am about the Roosevelt dime, but I am not. It is just plain more interesting. Perhaps it is because this series has at least two moderately scarce issues (1932-D and S). Perhaps it is because it has been around longer or just because it is larger. I do not know why, but I like this series and think that other collectors do too. More important, I do not think that it has been exploited, so if you are willing to do some work, you should be able to get ahead of the market.

Half Dollars:

Half dollars and dollars are probably the two most popular denominations to collect today. Part of the reason for this and the common factor between them is that their larger size allows for better designs. We have some beautiful dollars and halves.

Half dollars were introduced in 1794 along with the dollar and ahead of the dime and quarter. The early types—draped bust (1794–1807), capped bust (1807–1836), Liberty seated (1839–1891), and Barber or Liberty head (1892-1915)—parallel the corresponding smaller denominations with many varieties, low mintages, and scarce issues.

Again, if you will settle for well-worn examples, you can still obtain many of these beautiful coins at low prices.

The Liberty walking half dollar was introduced in 1916. Collectors call these beautiful coins "walk-

The beautiful seated Liberty design was issued 1839-1891.

The Liberty head half replaced the Liberty seated design in 1892.

ers." They circulated into the early 1960s, so many examples are available from the general public. The number of varieties is greatly reduced compared to the earlier types, but there are still many collecting challenges within the series. There are a few low mintages but no great rarities, and gorgeous examples of common, late dates can be purchased for modest amounts for type collections. However,

The walking Liberty half is one of our most popular coins.

Franklin half dollars are attractive and modestly priced.

many of the issues are very difficult to find in top condition.

The Franklin half dollar was issued 1948–1963. Franklin is the first non-president to have his portrait appear on a regular issue coin. (Several actual people posed for allegories used on coins, and many actual non-presidents have had their portraits on commemorative coins, as recently as 1995.)

The Franklin half is a beautiful coin that had a relatively short life and until recently was overlooked by many collectors. Even though the series has been studied and promoted in recent years, it is still a good place for you to start a collection. You can buy some nice uncirculated examples from the 1950s and 1960s at very low prices and the most expensive coin in the whole set can be bought for about $50 in uncirculated condition.

Everyone knows and loves the Kennedy half dollar. It is not nearly as beautiful as the Franklin or walking Liberty. It certainly is not scarce, but collectors and the general public like it. When it was introduced in 1964, everyone clamored to get one. If one was good, two were better, and 50 better still. Then the price of silver skyrocketed and silver was hoarded. Dimes, quarters, and walkers were sold and melted. Kennedys were mostly kept. The half dollar disappeared from circulation. It is hard to believe that before 1964 the half dollar was commonly used in commerce. In the 1980s and 1990s, between 30 and 40 million Kennedys are minted

The general public still hoards Kennedy half dollars.

every year, but where are they? People hoard them because they like them.

There is not a lot of diversity in the Kennedy series, but there is enough that you can have some fun with them for a while. There are some proof only issues and even a mint set-only issue and they are cheap.

Silver Dollars:

Silver dollars. Cart wheels. Carson City, San Francisco, Denver, the wild west. Mining. Everyone seems to love them. Several books have been written just about investing in silver dollars. These are in addition to several good books about the history and lore of our largest silver coin.

The silver dollar was introduced in 1794 and has had a checkered history. Flowing hair (1794–1795) and draped bust (1795–1804) dollars are classic designs of early coinage that deserve our admiration. The denomination was suspended after the 1803 date through 1840.

Mint records indicate that nearly 20,000 dollars were struck in 1804. However, it was the practice at the time to continue using dies until they wore out rather than waste them because the year changed. Therefore it is believed that those 20,000 dollars were dated 1803. However, there are a few 1804 dollars—the king of American coins, a coin of legendary proportions, with a history as good as Hollywood could create.

The silver dollar was introduced in 1794.

Actually, we do not know the whole story of the 1804 dollar. There is an entire book on this one coin and research is still uncovering new information. The essence of it is that the first of the coins were struck in 1834–35 for inclusion in some presentation sets. Within the next ten years a few more were made to meet collector demand. Many purists sneer that the 1804 silver piece is not even a coin because it was not actually issued, but no one can take away the luster that has developed over 175 years.

Liberty seated dollars (1840–1873) are beautiful. You should take the opportunity to study some uncirculated examples in an auction or dealer's display case, but even though there are relatively few varieties, there also are very few common dates. There is not much collecting to be done in seated dollars without some serious money.

The Morgan dollar (1878–1921) is a nice coin.

Liberty seated dollars are extremely beautiful in uncirculated condition.

More collectors specialize in the Morgan dollar than any other series.

In the 1960s you could order original mint bags of dollars from your bank. You could receive anything from the middle 1880s through the 1920s. It was amazing, but almost no one cared! Relatively few collectors collected them because the face value was too high.

Of course the removal of silver from our coins in 1965 changed that and silver dollars disappeared from circulation in the same way that the Kennedy half did.

Then two remarkable things happened that greatly expanded the number of coins available for collectors and the number of collectors for the coins. First, the United States treasury sold millions of silver dollars from its vaults. Secondly, the Laverne Redfield hoard was sold to the trade (see additional information in "the great collectors"). The increased supply made the demand go up! It was marketing brilliance that has had a profound and lasting effect on collecting.

Wonderful uncirculated examples of common dates can be found for very low prices. You can get a New Orleans coin for the same price as a Philadelphia and a Carson City for not too much more. Go ahead, you should have one for a type set. However, for a serious collection, I recommend almost anything else! These coins have been studied to death. More people specialize in the Morgan dollar than in any other coin series. Sure, more discoveries will be made and you could be the one to

The Peace dollar was introduced as a commemorative honoring the end of World War I.

make them, but it will be a lot easier in other areas.

The Peace dollar (1921–1935) was introduced as a commemorative honoring the end of World War I. As a "short series" existing for only a few years, it holds some promise as a place to start an interesting collection, but I find them uninspiring. You probably should obtain a nice example as a type and find somewhere else to specialize. Most of the comments regarding collecting of Morgan dollars apply to Peace dollars as well. There is one very interesting twist to the history of this coin.

In 1964 Congress authorized the coinage of this design again and over 300,000 pieces were struck with the 1964 date. Then the price of silver skyrocketed and the coins were melted before any were officially issued. Rumors persist that at least a few of these coins remain in private hands. It is likely that the treasury would deem these coins to be illegally held and seize any that appeared on the market. See the story of the 1933 double eagle below.

The Eisenhower dollar (1971–1978) is an interesting short series. There are no rarities, but there is enough variety to have some fun. There has been increasing interest in the Ikes, and if you like them, there can be little harm in building a set.

The Susan B. Anthony dollar (1979–1981) was an ill-fated attempt to introduce a real circulating dollar coin to commerce. The hearts of the proposers were in the right place, but it was an ill-conceived plan from the beginning.

It is obvious that the coin did not circulate. The most common reason given is that it was too close to the size of a quarter. The next reason given is that there was no room in cash registers. The last reason given is that many people did not like Anthony so they avoided the coin, although you seldom hear this reason stated publicly.

All of these reasons are wrong. Experienced numismatists at the time predicted the failure of the experiment. The bottom line is that when the population has the choice of a paper dollar and a base metal coin, it will take the paper money every time. Neither has an intrinsic value of any consequence and the paper money is easier to carry. A dollar coin will circulate when the dollar bill is discontinued.

From 1873 through 1885 a trade dollar was minted. This coin was not intended for domestic commerce, but for export as bullion. This is a fascinating coin that has not been fully studied although it has gained attention in the past few years. This is a great coin to study and I like it much better than the Morgan dollar, but you cannot assemble much of a collection without investing a substantial amount.

Silver bullion coins were created in 1986 and have been issued each year since. These pieces use A. A. Weinman's beautiful walking Liberty design for the obverse. These pieces are silver dollars only because they are made of silver and the government decreed them as dollar coins. They are actually silver ingots, but they are attractive and inexpensive enough that you may want to buy a few just because you like them.

Gold Coins:

The romance associated with the yellow metal is undeniable and its coinage has a compelling history. To hold a nineteenth century double eagle ($20) in your hand is to travel to another time by dream. In the 1950s, my mother took me to a coin store in a neighboring city. I was enthralled by

The $3 gold coin was one of the shortest lived coins (and denominations) in United States history.

large cents, 2¢ and 3¢ pieces, but I was stunned when the dealer showed a gold type set to an adult customer. I do not remember if that customer bought the set. I certainly did not have the courage even to ask to hold the set, but I will never forget the moment.

Although it is not likely that you will ever own a major collection of gold coins, it is possible to acquire a few pieces for a type set at fairly low prices. They are particularly modest if you consider that the bulk of the price of such a coin is in the gold bullion itself. You could melt it and sell it for about 75 percent of what you paid for it!

The lore of gold coins is sufficient to allow study for weeks, but the basics are not very difficult. An eagle was $10. We also had double, half, and quarter eagles. In addition to these coins we had $1 and $3 denominations. A $4 coin was also proposed and

This pattern was struck in 1879 for a proposed $4 coin.

Two designs were proposed for the $4 coin. Patterns of both are rare - and expensive.

patterns struck, but the denomination was never produced for circulation.

President Theodore Roosevelt took a special interest in our coinage. He persuaded the sculptor Augustus Saint-Gaudens to redesign our coins. Unfortunately, Saint-Gaudens died before completing the task, but he did complete designs for the eagle and double eagle. Most collectors consider the design of the double eagle to be our most beautiful coin. I consider that of his eagle to be even more beautiful.

In 1933 President Franklin Roosevelt took our money off the gold standard and outlawed private ownership of gold. This prohibition remained in effect until 1978. Although the public did not generally understand this, it was legal during the prohibition to own American gold coins as part of a collection.

Eagles and double eagles were struck in 1933. Only a few of the eagles were officially released before the presidential edict ended gold coinage. Therefore, these 1933 eagles are rare and expensive, as you might imagine. However, that is only a minor story compared to the double eagle. Since 1933 the government has steadfastly maintained that no 1933 double eagles were legally distributed and that therefore any in private hands were not legally held. Treasury agents have in fact confiscated 1933 double eagles. The collection of King Farouk of Egypt included one of these coins, but it

This $10 gold (eagle) was designed by famed sculptor Augustus Saint Gaudens.

was withdrawn from the sale of his collection at the request of the United States government. The disposition of the Farouk coin has not been reported since that time.

The story gets better. In the 1990s there is growing evidence that the treasury cannot support the position that all 1933 double eagles are illegally held. It may be necessary for an example to appear in the marketplace in order for a decision to be reached. That could be a risky proposition for the parties to such a sale, but it certainly would be interesting. I predict that within the next decade these coins will trade without interference by the government.

The 1933 double eagle illustrated on this book's cover is in the national collection at the Smithsonian Institution. Preparing this book gave me an excuse to research at the Smithsonian and I was allowed to hold this magnificent coin. For a lifelong collector, this was a remarkable moment.

Gold bullion coins were created in 1986 and have been issued each year since. These pieces use Augustus Saint-Gaudens' wonderful design (modified) from the 1907 double eagle for the obverse. Four different weight pieces are issued annually (.1oz., .25oz., .5oz., and 1 oz). They have face values of $5, $10, $25, and $50, but they are coins only because the government decreed them as coins. They are actually gold ingots, but they are attractive and inexpensive enough that you may want to buy a few just because you like them.

Commemorative Coins:

Commemoratives coins are very popular with collectors, and for good reason. Many of them were designed by top artists and are beautiful. Few are actually rare in the sense of classic coinages, but some have total mintages of only 10,000 and many individual issues have much lower mintages. Some have historic themes, but others, well, let us say that they left something to be desired.

When collectors say that they collect commemoratives, they generally mean the mostly noncirculating *silver* commemoratives of the 1892–1954 period. They may or may not include the corresponding gold issues in their collections.

All of this is to say that they generally exclude the so-called modern commemoratives (1982–present). Of course this attitude will change some day, and I have more to say on collecting these "modern" commemoratives below. For now I simply want to point out that even the definition of commemoratives that these collectors typically use is deficient. A quarter eagle was issued in 1848 to commemorate the California source of the gold. The design of the quarter was changed in 1932 to commemorate the 200th anniversary of Washington's birth and the design of the silver dollar was changed in 1921 to the Peace design to commemorate the peace after the "war to end all wars." There are other examples too, but the coins above are almost never included in commemorative collections. One of the key criteria for a commemorative coin to be popular with collectors is that it was (or was intended to be) a non-circulating coin. This is a curious situation, but it has prevailed for at least a few decades!

The coins that many collectors shun are collectively called modern commemoratives. There is no widely recognized term to describe what they do collect. Many of these collectors seem to be satisfied with "commemorative" as if the modern commemoratives are somehow something else. "Classic" is another word that is sometimes used.

The Columbian half dollar was released into circulation when it did not sell out.

That seems a little pompous, but for lack of anything better, we will use "classic."

The first United States non-circulating commemorative coins were produced in 1892 for the World's Columbian Exposition. Ironically, circulated examples of the 1893 Columbian 50¢ commemorative are among the most common in collections. This is because many were released into circulation when the entire mintage was not sold to the public. A 25¢ commemorative was also issued for the fair, but it is far from common in any condition.

From 1892 through 1954 many interesting (and a few decidedly uninteresting) commemoratives were issued. The system of selecting and issuing the commemoratives became so corrupted that all commemoratives were discontinued.

An interesting example is the 1936 commemorative issued for the centen-

This commemorative quarter was issued for the World's Columbian exposition in 1892. It is a key piece for collectors.

nial of Bridgeport, Connecticut. This is certainly a significant local event, but hardly seems like a matter for a commemorative coin. It gets even better. The obverse of the coin has a large portrait of none other than P. T. Barnum! He certainly would have smiled knowing that the few people who actually bought one of these coins paid $2 for the 50¢ piece! Of course today you would have to pay substantially more for a nice example.

The Panama-Pacific International Exposition was held in California in 1915. Commemorative coins were struck to raise money for the occasion. The set of coins was the most extensive until the United States began issuing coins for the Olympics in 1983. The Pan–Pacific set consists of a silver 50¢ and gold $1, $2.50, and two different $50 coins! Yes, $50 commemoratives in 1915. Even more amazing, the $50 came in a rather traditional round design and a variation of the same design in an octagonal format. This is a wonderful set from the point of view of collectors in the 1990s. Collectors did not think that it was so great in 1915, and only a few of the $50 pieces were sold (483 and 645 respectively for the round and octagonal).

I have two personal stories about these coins that might make a few interesting points. In 1972 I was a soldier getting ready to go to Vietnam. I was a keen, but not necessarily advanced collector.

I went to a very small coin show somewhere in North Carolina. I saw a set of the Pan-Pacific silver and gold commemoratives on display in a beautiful copper frame. These copper frames are often called "original copper frames," implying that the sets were issued that way. This is not the case, but the set in this frame is stunning. I had never seen such a set. I guess that I might have read about it, but having never seen one, I loved it.

In the little time that I had before going to Vietnam, I studied this set. I found that I could buy one of these sets for about $6,000 or $7,000, assuming that I could find one for sale of course. I certainly could not afford such a price, but I could have raised most of it and financed the rest.

Instead of trying to buy a set, I decided that I would save my money and if I made it back from Vietnam, I would buy myself one of these sets. During my year in Vietnam, I not only saved $6,000, but also thought a lot about that set.

When I made it home in 1973, I looked into buying a set. But by then the price had gone to $12,000. I was ready to pay $7,000, but that was not enough. Again, I could have raised some more money and financed the rest to pay $12,000, but I could not bear to pay so much when only a year before I could have had it for $7,000.

The next one I saw for sale was in an auction. It sold for over $100,000. Of course I was willing to pay $12,000 then!

Since that time $50 Pan-Pacifics and sets (not necessarily in the copper frames) have been reasonably available and the prices have even fluctuated, but they have never gone down to anything approaching something that I could even finance. I have never owned a Pan-Pacific set and probably never will.

There are several lessons here. The first is that what I did is called chasing. Most of us have done it with automobiles or something, and occasionally, it pays dividends because the price goes down. But only occasionally. If the item is rare and desirable, and the market for it and similar items has been stable, the trend will be up.

When the price was $7,000 and then $12,000, it was difficult or harder to find a set. That is an indicator that an item is underpriced or at least not overpriced. When the set sold for $100,000, it was easy to find a set. This usually happens when a price goes up fast. Collectors who bought a set at $7,000 were happy to keep it when they thought that it would only sell for $12,000. When they learned that it might sell for $100,000, many of them decided that they had owned it long enough!

Chasing is not fun.

Another Pan-Pacific story does not have a moral

that is clear to me, but it is too good not to tell. John Pittman is one of the great collectors of this (or any) century. He told me this story. He had a $50 Pan-Pacific for sale. I doubt if it was from his collection. Perhaps he was selling it for a friend. Anyway, he approached a dealer he thought might be interested. John gave the dealer the coin for examination. The dealer liked the coin and the two of them entered negotiations.

During the negotiations, the dealer mentioned several times that if John had the original box (not copper frame), the dealer could pay more. As they agreed on price X, the dealer even said that if John had the box he could pay Y, which was substantially more. I guess that this was his way of justifying a somewhat low price for the coin. With only a small smile, John said that he would accept Y and pulled the box from his pocket!

As we have seen in the above stories, we had gold as well as silver commemoratives during the 1892–1954 period. Actually, there were relatively few issues and if it were not for the $50 Pan-Pacifics, most people could eventually build a type set. However, there are more opportunities with modern gold commemoratives.

Modern Commemoratives:

In 1982 the practice of issuing commemoratives was reinstituted, much to the glee of collectors. Today most of those same collectors feel that the abuses of the 1950s are again in play. Usually these post-1980 commemoratives are called modern commemoratives and are sneered at by collectors of "classic" commemoratives and other collectors too.

The first example is the 1982 Washington half dollar. These coins were issued by the mint at about $12. They can now be purchased in the coin market for about $4. In an ironic twist, George Washington was honored on our first commemorative dollar coin in 1900, where he shared the honor with Lafayette. It was not until 1932 that Washington appeared alone on a coin. The 1932 quarter was intended to be a commemorative but was continued in 1934 as a regular issue piece.

The 1995 Special Olympics dollar commemorative is another point of contention. This coin features a large portrait of Eunice Shriver. Eunice Shriver has done much to promote the Special Olympics, but she is also a member of the Kennedy family and a living person. George Washington started a tradition of not having living persons on American coins when he refused to allow his portrait on our first coins. There has never been a major exception like this one.

Add to these problems the fact (or opinion) that the commemorative coin designs have been generally uninspired or poor and you have a bad situation. Many or most serious collectors suggest that all of this means that you should not collect "modern" commemoratives. I feel that this reaction is much too strong. I really like the 1982 Washington half dollar and think that it is a steal at $4. I like to give them as gifts. I even break them out of the plastic and carry them in my pocket. I like a few others, too. In addition, a medal was issued with the 1994 World War II commemorative coins. It was issued in a special holder with a half dollar. I procrastinated in ordering one of these and by the time

The 1995 Special Olympics one dollar commemorative has been very controversial. It is typical of modern commemoratives in that regard.

that I tried, it was sold out. Furthermore, it has been quite difficult to locate any of these medals since then. Where did they go?

The point is that you should make your own decision about each issue and if there is one that you like, go ahead and buy it. In most cases, however, you will be much better off to buy it from a coin dealer a year after the issue rather than directly from the mint!

Here are lists of "classic" and modern commemoratives, with the theme of each one so that you can see if there are any that particularly appeal to you.

COMMEMORATIVE HALF DOLLAR THEMES 1892-1954 WITH DATES

Alabama Centennial, 1921

Albany, New York, Charter, 1936

Battle of Antietam, 1937

Arkansas Centennial, 1935–1939

Arkansas Centennial (with Senator Joseph Robinson), 1936

Bay Bridge (Oakland-San Francisco) Opening, 1936

Daniel Boone Bicentennial, 1934–1938

Bridgeport, Connecticut, Centennial, 1936

California Diamond Jubilee, 1925

Carver (George Washington)-Washington (Booker T.), 1951–54

Cincinnati Music Center, 1936

Cleveland Great Lakes Exposition, 1936

Columbia, South Carolina, Sesquicentennial, 1936

Columbian Exposition, 1892–93

Connecticut Tercentenary, 1935

Delaware Tercentenary, 1936

Elgin, Illinois, Centennial, 1936

Battle of Gettysburg, 1936

Grant Memorial, 1922

Hawaii Sesquicentennial, 1928

Hudson, New York, Sesquicentennial, 1935
Huguenot-Walloon Tercentenary, 1924
Illinois Centennial, 1918
Iowa Centennial, 1946
Lexington-Concord Sesquicentennial, 1925
Long Island Tercentenary, 1936
Lynchburg, Virginia, Sesquicentennial, 1936
Maine Centennial, 1920
Maryland Tercentenary, 1934
Missouri Centennial, 1921
Monroe Doctrine Centennial, 1923
New Rochelle, New York, 1938
Norfolk, Virginia, Bicentennial, 1936
Oregon Trail Memorial, 1926–1939
Pan-Pacific Exposition, 1915
Pilgrim Tercentenary, 1920-21
Rhode Island Tercentenary, 1936
Roanoke Island, North Carolina, 1937
San Diego, California, Pacific Exposition, 1935-36
Sesquicentennial of American Independence, 1926
Old Spanish Trail, 1935
Stone Mountain Memorial, 1925
Texas Centennial, 1934–38
Fort Vancouver Centennial, 1925
Vermont Sesquicentennial, 1927
Booker T. Washington Memorial, 1946–51
Wisconsin Territorial Centennial, 1936
York County, Maine, Tercentenary, 1936

OTHER CLASSIC COMMEMORATIVE SILVER COINS

Isabella quarter, 1893
Lafayette dollar, 1900

CLASSIC GOLD COMMEMORATIVES

Grant Memorial, $1, 1922
Lewis and Clark Exposition, $1, 1904–05
Louisiana Purchase Exposition, $1, 1903
McKinley Memorial, $1, 1916–17

Pan Pacific Exposition, $1, $2.50, $50, 1915
Sesquicentennial of American Independence,
$2.50, 1926

MODERN COMMEMORATIVES

The trend with modern commemoratives is to produce them in sets with denominations and to produce the sets of gold and silver coins in both proof and business strikes. The Olympic games have become by far the most popular or at least prolific subject matter for United States commemorative coins.

As described above, most serious collectors shun the modern commemoratives. They frequently describe the coins as junk, and with some justification I must say. They have too frequently honored marginal events with uninspired (at best) designs with mintages that are too high at prices equally too high. This is in spite of the fact that there have been no circulating commemoratives since the 1976 bicentennial coins.

Bill of Rights, 50¢, $1, $5 gold, 1993
Civil War, Preservation of Historic Battlefields,
    50¢, $1, $5 gold, 1995
Christopher Columbus Quincentenary, 50¢, $1,
    $5 gold, 1992
Constitutional Bicentennial, $1, $5 gold, 1987
Congress Bicentennial, 50¢, $1, $5 gold, 1989
Eisenhower Centennial, $1, 1990
50th Anniversary of World War II, 1991–1995,
    50¢, $1, $5 gold (and medal), 1993
Thomas Jefferson, 1993, $1
Korean War Memorial, $1, 1991
Mount Rushmore, 50¢, $1, $5 gold, 1991
Olympics
    Atlanta, Georgia, 50¢, $1, $5 gold, 1995–96
    Barcelona, Spain, and Albertville, France,
    50¢, $1, $5 gold, 1992
    Los Angeles, 1983–84, $1, $10 gold
    Seoul, $1, $5 gold, 1988

Special Olympics (Eunice Shriver) $1, 1995
Statue of Liberty, 50¢, $1, $5 gold, 1986
Tribute to American Prisoners of War, $1, 1994
United Service Organizations (USO), $1, 1991
Vietnam War Memorial, $1, 1994
George Washington, 50¢, 1982
White House 200th Anniversary, $1, 1992
Women Veterans, $1, 1994
World Cup Tournament, 50¢, $1, $5 gold, 1994

Commemorative coins, while extremely popular, have had more and wider market cycles than any other series of coins. This should not dissuade you. In fact if you like these commemoratives, it should encourage you. The lesson from it is buy commemoratives when they are down. Although it may not seem like it, when commems are hot, the prices almost surely will go down. Buy when they do.

Errors:
Coins that were not manufactured to the normal standard of quality are errors and are popular with many collectors. Some amazing errors exist. Examples are coins struck on the wrong planchet (coin blank) such as a 1¢ piece on a dime planchet!

Clipped planchets are not complete discs. They have metal missing from the time that they were manufactured. The missing portion may be curved, straight, ragged, or elliptical. Sometimes these planchets are then struck creating interesting errors.

Off-center coins were stuck so that part of the design is missing from the planchet. A corresponding part of the planchet does not have any design. Coins that are only struck slightly off center, with none of the design missing, are usually not considered to have any special significance. Those with nearly all of the impression missing are generally the most desirable, but modern cents more than 50 percent off center are actually quite common and command little premium. The most desirable are those with substantial portions of the design missing, but with the date and mint mark present.

Blank planchets sometimes find their way out of the mint without having been struck at all. Blanks are prepared in two steps. First they are punched from a strip of metal, then the edges are milled to upset the rim for striking. Therefore, it is possible to have blanks with or without upset rim. Those without the rim are generally more desirable. Some obscure—and interesting—blanks exist. From 1942 to 1945 the composition of the 5¢ piece was changed removing the nickel and adding silver. A few of these blanks exist, but they are not easily recognized as being different from "normal" 5¢ blanks. Of course, these silver blanks are much more rare, desirable, and valuable.

Sometimes a coin is struck more than one time, occasionally several times. Each successive strike leaves a partial impression. The most desirable multiple strike has several strikes and a visible date and mint mark.

Varieties:

Some coins exist with small differences in the details of the designs. These differences are called varieties. These coins are not errors, even though they may have been the result of a mistake by a worker at the mint.

It is possible to identify the actual dies from which coins were stuck by carefully studying the coin. Relatively few dies were used for many nineteenth century coins, so it is possible to determine every die and die combination used to mint a given coin or series of coins. Potentially every die combination creates a collectable variety and books have been written about the die varieties of several different series. The authors of these books assign numbers to each variety to make it easier to identify them. The varieties are then called by the name of the author and the number like Overton 25 (for bust dollars) and Sheldon 1 (for large cents). While these varieties are the realm of the specialist, you will see such designations in auction catalogs and sales lists.

A *pattern* is a trial strike of a proposed design. The mintages of patterns are very small, making them rare in most cases. A surprising number of nineteenth century pattern coins may be found in collections, but they are still rare. Technically an *essay* is a trial of an unadopted design. A *trial* can be a strike of just part of a design or any other experimental product. Frequently the term pattern is used to describe patterns, essays, or trials. You should read about patterns in auction catalogs and study a few pieces at an auction viewing. Actually, patterns are not particularly expensive considering their rarity, but you should study the specialized literature before you think about venturing into the world of "what might have been."

Medals and Other Things:

The United States Mint produces more than coins for circulation. We have already discussed pattern and proof coins that are manufactured at the mint; it also produces coins for foreign governments, medals, bullion coins and ingots, and military and civilian decorations. The degree to which these items are included in a collection of American coins depends upon the interests of the collectors. Indeed, some specialists are not even aware of some of the obscure products.

The United States mints have minted coins for many different foreign governments at various times. The height of this work was during World War II when this mint work helped the war effort by helping the Allies overcome economic and manufacturing difficulties. Even closer to home, coins were struck in the continental United States 1903–1945 for the Philippines which were under United States sovereignty. These coins included 1936 commemorative coins. One of these has a portrait of Presidents Roosevelt and Quezon. Additional coins were struck in Manila during this period, so there is a strong argument that the

Manila mint should be included in any discussion of United States mints.

You probably saw General Colin Powell being presented a gold medal for his distinguished service during the Gulf War. It is not likely that you gave it a second thought at the time, but the unique gold medal was prepared at the United States mint for presentation to General Powell. This is a practice that dates to the eighteenth century; now the general public can purchase bronze versions of this gold medal at a nominal price.

The mint also routinely prepares medals as part of ongoing series. As you might expect, there is a set of presidential medals. These are large (3") medals featuring portraits of the presidents. These medals can be purchased from the mint in their full or reduced size. Other series include directors of the mint and secretaries of the treasury.

Bullion Coins:

The United States began issuing silver and gold bullion coins called eagles in 1986. These were to compete with the South African Krugerrand and Canadian Maple Leaf coins. The coins have been successful and have been issued each year since introduction. Although most collectors do not have much interest in these bullion pieces, they are interesting in several ways.

The pieces are officially coins because they were properly issued by the government and have face values. However, they are sold well above face value so that they never have circulated and it is unlikely that they ever will. It would be an interesting experiment to try to redeem a worn and dirty silver eagle.

Classic designs of proven popularity were used for the obverses of these coins. The gold coins used a modified version of the beautiful Saint-Gaudens double eagle, while the silver coins used the Weinman's walking Liberty design (used previously for half dollars 1916–1946).

The silver eagles are 1 oz. silver pieces with a

face value of $1. The gold pieces have interesting denominations: $50, $25, $10, and $5, which wiegh 1oz., .5oz., .25oz., and .1 oz. of gold respectively. Even though most collectors do not consider these to be real coins, the $25 is a denomination that has never been used except for these coins. You can probably win more than a few wagers surrounding the idea that the United States has issued coins of this denomination.

In 1907 when the Saint-Gaudens design was introduced, the date was in roman numerals. This was discontinued that same year, but it was adopted again in 1986, but discontinued again in 1992.

In 1995 the mint began selling jewelry and other items made from its minted products. Most collectors are amused, bewildered, or even angry that the mint has gotten involved in such merchandising. Not much information has been published about the actual manufacturing of these products, but they probably were not produced at the mint. As amazing as it may seem, it is possible that a century from now collectors will prize these items that we criticize.

Tokens:

Tokens are issued as substitutes for genuine money by agencies that do not have the authority to issue real coins. Therefore, the United States mint does not issue tokens, though many people argue that it has produced tokens exclusively since silver was removed from our coins in 1965. Transportation tokens for buses and subways are the most common tokens today, and it should not come as a surprise that people collect transportation tokens.

There are several periods of United States history with economic difficulties that generated the widespread use of private tokens as substitutes for coinage. The first was the colonial period. Tokens from this period were very close to coins in form and function. There was very little or no coinage, so today these tokens are highly prized by collectors. (See the Redbook for good descriptions and listings of these tokens.)

The Civil War created economic chaos in the North and the South. A partial solution to coin shortages in the North was private tokens. Merchants issued these tokens to make small change thus allowing commerce to continue. Of course they made a profit on the tokens themselves while they were at it—and they even added their own advertising message or political slogan to the token.

Richard Doty of the Smithsonian Institution's Department of Numismatics estimates that over 11,000 different tokens were issued and that something like 25 million tokens were issued in all. Not surprisingly, you can collect Civil War tokens for a long time without getting them all. Even better, you can obtain many different pieces of these historic Civil War relics at nominal prices.

While many Civil War tokens are common and available at low prices, there are of course better items that sell for substantially higher prices. As a group the tokens created by John Gault fall into this category. Gault created a token that included an actual United States postage stamp inside the token and under a transparent cover. These encased stamps were gladly accepted by the public because they clearly were worth the price of the stamp. Gault would have lost money on each token except that the back of the token was available for advertising that he sold very successfully.

Of course the government was jealous of the money that Gault was making and stepped in to stop his enterprise. Today Gault's encased stamps are very popular and the subject of an entire book. Although they are much more expensive than the routine Civil War trade token, Gault's encased stamps are not extraordinarily expensive.

Still More Things:

There seems to be no end of interesting things for your American coin collection. A friend of mine collects coin envelopes used by famous dealers. B. Max Mehl and other famous dealers had their name and address printed on the coin envelopes that they used. These envelopes are not easy to find. They are themselves documents in the history of collecting, and most of them have annotations of what coins they contained. This information was usually written by the dealer, and the buyer of the coin frequently then added a date and purchase price. Collectors today sometimes get these envelopes when they buy coins that came from an old-time collection. It is not unusual to have an envelope from a classic dealer that was owned by a great collector from fifty years ago and sold with the same coin by one of today's major dealers or auctioneers.

I have started a collection of sales literature from the United States mint. While there is a wide array of items and an seemingly unending supply, it is difficult if not impossible to find such materials from just a few years ago. I expect to have fun with the collection and the price is certainly right!

Many people collect numismatic literature. Books, auction catalogs, magazines, and even dealers' price lists are collected. The real proof of this is that there are now dealers who trade exclusively in antique numismatic literature.

Armand Champa is a real gentleman and keen collector. He sold his major coin collection some years ago and concentrated his efforts on collecting coin books. In 1994 and 1995 he sold his collection in a series of auctions. The total sale price was well over $1 million.

The Redbook is so popular among collectors that a price guide for its fifty annual editions is included in the book itself. Besides the fact that these books now have value and are fun to collect, having a complete set or partial set can also be useful. Obviously, it can be interesting and nostalgic to see what the price was on a coin in a given year or even to chart the annual values over the entire run of the catalog. It can also be important to know what the state of the hobby was at a given time. When were major varieties added to the listings in the Redbook?

Probably the most prized periodical is *The Numismatist*. Starting in 1890, over a hundred years of the history of the hobby are recorded in these pages. The early years are rare and demand high prices, but you can obtain the past forty or fifty years at very modest prices, and they too contain a lot of history.

In the finest cherry picking tradition it is possible to find old editions of the Redbook, *The Numismatist*, and many other very good antique numismatic literature in used book shops, antique shops, estate auctions, and the like.

Colonial Coins:

The history of United States coins starts with the colonies. Benjamin Franklin, Paul Revere and others whom we recognize as great patriots and founding fathers were personally involved with the development of our coinage during this period.

Coins or tokens were issued in most of the colonies. Without doubt the most famous is the Massachusetts Pine Tree Shilling. This is a wonderfully historic and even beautiful coin. To make matters even better for the beginning collector, it is not outrageously rare or expensive.

Many of the other colonial coins are rare, some are obscure, but they are all fascinating. After the colonial period, patterns were struck for the Continental Congress. Even if you cannot collect these coins, you should read about them and take the opportunity to study the illustrations in auction catalogs or books. Better yet, you can examine some of the actual coins at major coin shows and auctions.

FAMOUS COLLECTORS

Collectors are the heart of collecting. In the history of collecting there have been many great collectors. It has been said that numismatics is the king of hobbies and the hobby of kings. Kings Victor Emmanuel of Italy and Farouk of Egypt both built spectacular collections. The sale of the Farouk collection was one of the great events in the history of twentieth century collecting.

We tend to think of these as being from the past and distant past, but this is far from true. Great collectors are building collections today. Below are capsule stories about some of the great late and current collectors.

Louis Eliasberg assembled the only "complete" collection of United States coinage. We think of this an impossible task today because of the high values involved, and it probably is impossible. However, it was a monumental task even for someone who started much earlier in this century. Eliasberg bought single coins and entire collections to get the coins that he needed for his collection. He sold duplicate coins that he acquired through the same auction firms that he patronized to purchase coins. On at least one occasion he used an assumed name to sell duplicates.

After Eliasberg died in 1976, his collection was displayed at the United States mint in Philadelphia and then at other venues around the country. In 1982 this gold collection was auctioned, but his name was never mentioned in the catalog.

LaVere Redfield from Reno was a speculator in real estate and a very wealthy man in 1974. He was also known for being a bit eccentric. He had a hoard of over 400,000 silver dollars. These silver dollars had been obtained from banks at face value. The story goes that IRS agents found this hoard in his basement behind a fake wall. Allegedly a note on top of the pile of bags said "Don't let the IRS know about this." Whether or not this part of the story is true, it was an amazing hoard. After several dealers were contacted about the coins, a nasty court battle ensued over who could buy the dollars at what price. In the end A-Mark Corporation bought the hoard for $7.3 million!

Byron Reed was a wealthy collector from Omaha. In 1890 he bought the Parmelee 1804 dollar for $570. When he died in 1891 his collection included about 10,000 coins, tokens, medals, and pieces of paper money. It was valued at $2 million at the time. Reed left it to the city of Omaha.

His collection was displayed rather routinely until 1930 when an attempted robbery made the custodians remove it from public view. Since then parts of it have been on display, but not the entire collection. In 1995 further controversy developed when the city decided to sell part of the collection in order to finance a better facility that would then be home for the balance of the collection.

B. Max Mehl was the greatest showman in numismatics. In 1903 he began to run advertisements in *The Numismatist*. They ran uninterrupted for fifty years. His *Star Rare Coin Encyclopedia* had a circulation of 70,000 in the 1920s. He issued at least seventy-five fixed price lists and conducted over 120 auctions (184,000 lots) many of which included great rarities. He advertised everywhere: magazines, match book covers, newspapers, and radio. He reportedly spent $100,000 per year for advertising. The advertisement that made him famous was to pay $50 for a 1913 Liberty nickel. In 1928 he had 128,000 mail order inquiries and made 30,000 shipments!

Amon Carter and Amon Carter, Jr., amassed great and vast collections. Jerry Buss is a well-known personality. He owns the Los Angeles Lakers. He is also a keen coin collector. He points out that he has made a fortune in business and collects coins for fun.

John Pittman is the dean of collectors. He collects just about everything: coins, medals, tokens, paper money, and more. He was a hardworking family man when he started. Seventy-some years later he has one of the finest collections in the world. Unfortunately, no report has been published of the contents of his collection, but it is awesome. Pittman has received virtually every honor in numismatics.

As the author of the Redbook, Richard Yeoman may have had more influence on coin collecting in the United States than any other single person. Of course this book has been a great and important book for numismatics, but it has also been a phenomenal success as a publishing venture. It is one of the best-selling books of all time. In fifty editions it has sold many millions of copies. Yeoman was a pen name for Richard S. Yeo.

Pedigrees describe the lineage of a coin. They can be very interesting and even increase the value of a coin. The following example reported by Kari Stone in the October 1995 *COINage* magazine demonstrates many things about the history, lore, and workings of collectors, and the market. This pedigree also reads like a who's who of numismatics.

The 1861 Paquet-reverse Liberty head double eagles are some of the most mysterious—and mystical—of American coins. They have been called patterns by some and unadopted regular issues by others. The two known examples were probably produced after January 1861 from a rejected reverse design.

One of the coins was for sale in 1995 for $1.3 million. It is known as the Norweb piece because it was owned by the famed collectors Ambassador R. Henry and Emery May Norweb. The coin's pedigree is extensive and quite impressive. It reads like a roster of hall of fame collectors.

The coin first appeared in an 1865 W. Elliot Woodward sale, to which it had been consigned either by William A. Lilliendahl or Colin Lightbody. At a time when most double eagles were bringing little more than face value, the coin brought $37. The buyer is said to have been George F. Seavey, who sold it in 1873 to Lorin G. Parmelee. The Paquet double eagle was then sold at auction in 1890 by the New York Coin and Stamp Co. for $44. It appeared again two years later in the same company's sale of the Woodside Collection, where it brought a lower price, $37.50.

The Chapman Brothers auctioned the coin in the sale of the M. A. Brown collection in 1897. Multimillionaire and collector extraordinare Virgil M. Brand bought it for $52.50. After Brand's death, the coin passed in 1932 to his brother Armin, who consigned it in 1936 to Burdette G. Johnson of the St. Louis Stamp and Coin Co. Johnson bought the coin himself for $500, and sold it in 1943 to Fred C. C. Boyd for $650. Boyd turned around and sold the Paquet double eagle for $1,250 to Abe Kosoff, who, with his partners Robert Friedberg and Hans M. F. Schulman, sold it to none other than King Farouk of Egypt—for $3,250.

After Farouk was driven into exile, the coin was sold in the 1954 Palace Collection Sale for $1,170.30 to David Spink, acting as agent for Charles Wormser and John J. Ford (New Netherlands Coin Co.). Wormser and Ford then sold the 1861 double eagle for $5,000 to Ambassador and Mrs. Norweb. The coin remained with the Norwebs until the late 1980s, when their collection was sold at auctions by Bowers and Merena.

Acting on behalf of a private investor, Manfra, Tordella and Brookes purchased the coin at the November 1988 sale for $660,000. Seven years later, the coin was obtained—for an undisclosed sum—by Spectrum Numismatics International. This firm then offered the coin for sale in 1995 for $1.3 million.

The pedigree of the second 1861 Paquet-Reverse Liberty head double eagle is less star studded, but in its own way is more intriguing. The coin "disappeared" from numismatic sight about 1877. Possibly it was spent. It was not seen again until it was recovered from European bullion reserves in the 1960s. Exhibiting many contact marks and wear from brief circulation, it is held in a Dallas bank as part of the Browning Collection.

THE INSTANT EXPERT'S COLLECTOR'S GUIDE

Organizations

The **American Numismatic Association** (ANA) is the mother of clubs. It is the largest numismatic organization in the world. It maintains a large headquarters in Colorado Springs with a museum, gift shop, and library. It also publishes a monthly magazine, and offers many other services. Most of these services are available by mail. Some new collectors think that the $30 or so membership fee would be better spent on coins. I recommend that the order of priority for spending is: 1) literature, 2) memberships, 3) coins. Once you join, make it a point to use the library.

The American Numismatic Association frequently has free memberships available for collectors under 18, and the regular dues for these young collectors are only $11. If you or a member of your family qualify, call the membership department and inquire. Tell them that you

Workmen install a new sign for the American Numismatic Association as Ken Hallenbeck presents a check from the Louis M. Reagen Foundation to executive director Bob Leuver (center) for erection of the sign.

read about it in the Instant Expert guide, but do not tell anyone else! Here is another little-known tip. The ANA has a toll-free number for membership services: (800) 367-9723.

The **American Numismatic Society** (ANS) is located in New York City. It has a museum with exhibits open to the public and the world's largest numismatic library. Although this is not a circulating library, it is open to the public five days a week and is a great resource for collectors who can spend time in New York City.

The **National Numismatic Collection**, the nation's coin collection, is housed at the Smithsonian Institution. It includes the former mint collection and many thousands of other items. You should visit the gallery in the Museum of American History the next time that you are in Washington, D.C.

The **Professional Numismatists Guild, Inc.** (PNG) is an association of dealers. It was formed in 1950 by the late Abe Kosoff. He wanted to create an organization to help collect debts. In the first year twenty-five dealers "signed up." Since that time it has grown to a powerful trade organization

The headquarters of the American Numismatic Association is in the shadow of Pike's Peak in Colorado Springs, Colorado. The association is the largest of its kind in the world and offers many benefits to members.

of more than 500 members. It sponsors a few coin shows each year and conducts other programs promoting collecting. It publishes an important directory of its members. Write PNG, Box 430, Van Nuys, CA 91408.

HELP IN PRINT

The Guidebook of United States Coins by R. S. Yeoman, Ken Bresset, editor, known universally as the Redbook, is a remarkable publication. It has been issued annually since 1946 and is one of the best-selling books in American book publishing. In spite of the proliferation of other price guides, newsletters, periodicals, and computer networks, the Redbook is still widely used by beginners and advanced collectors and dealers. The book combines a tremendous amount of technical data about all American coins as well as a value listing in a wonderfully succinct format. The book is even inexpensive. Every household should have at least one copy.

Walter Breen was one of the great numismatists of the twentieth century and the author of many articles and books. His crowning achievement was

Walter Breen's Complete Encyclopedia of U.S. and Colonial Coins. This is a great book. It seems a little expensive when you are first starting, but you will love the book and find it indispensable if you pursue American coins. Try borrowing a copy from you local library (do not forget to ask about interlibrary loan if necessary). It is also available from the American Numismatic Association library.

Silver and Gold Commemorative Coins by Walter Breen and Anthony Swiatek is the definitive study of American commemorative coins. It has all of the detailed information that you could possibly want on commemorative coins and is both interesting and entertaining to boot.

Since 1960, Amos Press of Sidney, Ohio, has been publishing *Coin World* on a weekly basis. Every week it includes news, features, trends, and advertising—lots and lots of advertising. Beginning collectors will find the advertising as interesting as the editorial material in most issues. This is a tribute to the advertisers, not a criticism of the news and feature writers. The success of the paper has gone up and down with the coin market and is reflected in the number of pages published each week. Indeed some market watchers gauge the trend of the market by the number of pages in and the number of subscribers to *Coin World.* Trends listings are included in every issue.

Chet Krause made a bold move when he started *Numismatic News* in 1952. The weekly newspaper that he literally put together on his kitchen table while he continued to work as a carpenter has grown into a publishing powerhouse. Krause now publishes numismatic catalogs, at least five numismatic periodicals, and publications in other fields as well. *Instant Expert* tip -> you can get a free copy of *Numismatic News* by writing Krause Publications and telling them that you saw the notice in the Instant Expert.

Coins magazine is the monthly magazine published by Krause Publications.

COINage has the largest circulation of any

numismatic publication because it is a very good magazine. It includes information and advertising for beginners along with plenty of interesting material for advanced collectors. The editors of *COINage* have agreed to send you a free sample if you mention the Instant Expert when you write!

The Numismatist is the monthly journal of the American Numismatic Association. In addition to association news, the magazine includes articles on a wide variety of topics of interest to numismatists. You will receive this after you join the association.

The *Coin Dealer Newsletter* is known as the Gray Sheet because of the color of its paper. It is the only really important newsletter in the trade. Everyone knows the Sheet and everyone who is seriously into the market uses the Sheet. It is published weekly by the *Coin Dealer Newsletter*, Box 7939, Torrance, CA 90504. It has been so successful that it has spawned a family of related newsletters.

DIRECTORIES

Shops

It is fun to visit coin shops! Although there are not nearly as many congenial coin shops in America as there once were, there still are many such shops. In these shops you can see, hold, examine, and buy many interesting and a few rare coins. In most of them you can engage in some conversation and in a few of them you can still get a cup of coffee.

I have listed a few shops here that are known to meet the ideals described above. I have been to these places of business or talked with those who have. Even though I can recommend them, you should call ahead. Often shops close for or at least send their inventories to shows. Also of course, they may have moved or stopped selling retail. Call first.

I cannot emphasize enough that you should read the publications mentioned throughout the *Instant Expert* and the telephone book to find other shops in your area or areas you may visit.

CALIFORNIA

The Coin Broker
91 Town and Country
Village
Palo Alto, CA 94301 (415)
323-8101

Jack H. Beymer
737 N. Coddingtown
Center
Santa Rosa, CA 95401
(707) 544-1621

COLORADO

**Ken Hallenbeck Coin
Gallery**
711 N. Nevada Ave.
Colorado Springs, CO
80903-1007
(719) 634-3313

FLORIDA

**Smith and Daughter,
Inc.**
2510 Biscayne Blvd.
Miami, FL 33137
(305) 573-1200

ILLINOIS

Harlan J. Berk, Ltd
31 N. Clark Street
Chicago, IL
(312) 609-0016

**Larry Whitlow, Galleria
Unique**
1 Lincoln Center #101
Oakbrook Terrace, IL
60181
(708) 916-2646

**Rarcoa (Rare Coin
Company of America,
Inc.)**
6262 South Route 83
Willowbrook, IL 60514
(708) 654-2580

KANSAS

S & S Coins
311 South 5th Street
Leavenworth, KS 66048
(913) 682-5574

MASSACHUSETTS

J. J. Teaparty, Inc.
51 Bromfield Street
Boston, MA 02108
(800) 343-6412

MARYLAND

Julian Leidman
940 Wayne Avenue
Silver Spring, MD 20910
(301) 585-8467

MONTANNA

Wayne Miller Coins
303 Fuller Ave.
Helena, MT 59601
(406) 442-0713

NEBRASKA

**Virg Marshall III, Inc.,
"The Penny Merchant"**
116 West "D" Street
Wymore, NE 68466
(402) 645-3342

NEVADA

Silver State Coin & Bullion
44 West First Street
Reno, NV 89501
(702) 322-4166

NEW YORK

Paul J. Bosco
1050 Second Avenue Store #89
New York, NY 10022
(212) 758-2646

Stacks
123 W. 57th St.
New York, NY 10019
(212) 582-2580

OHIO

Allens
399 S. State Street
Westerville, OH 43081
(614) 882-3937

Coin Shop
6841 Pearl Road
Middleburg Heights
(Cleveland area) OH 44130
(216) 884-0701

Vintage Coins and Cards
3509 Briarfield Boulevard
Maumee, OH 43537
(419) 865-2646

PENNSYLVANIA

Century Coins
4628 Clairton Blvd. (Rt 51 S)
Pittsburgh, PA 15222
(412) 882-6900

The Coin Exchange
143 6th Street
Pittsburgh, PA 15233
(412) 261-9000

Ossie's Coin Ship
1007 Hamilton Street
Allentown, PA 18101
(215) 433-4474

TEXAS

Garland Coin Shop
607 W. Main Street
Garland, TX
(214) 276-1773

R. E. Wallace Stamp and Coin
6th and Weatherford Streets
Fort Worth, TX 76102
(817) 338-4631

UTAH

All About Coins
1123 E. 2100 St.
Salt Lake City, UT 84106
(801) 467-8636

WASHINGTON

Pinnacle Rarities
10116 36th Avenue Court SW, Suite 310
Tacoma, WA 98499
(800) 432 6467

Rare Coin Galleries of Seattle
1416 Third Avenue
Seattle, WA 98101
(206) 624-4440

Seattle Coin Shop
316 Virginia Street
Seattle, WA 98101
(206) 448-2646

Tacoma Mall Boulevard Coin and Stamp
5225 Tacoma Mall Blvd.
#E101
Tacoma, WA 98409
(206) 472-9632

WISCONSIN

Bob's Coins
8307 W. Becher St.
Milwaukee, WI 53219
(424) 541-8650

Fox Valley Coin Exchange
Dept N11, 103 E. Kimberly Ave.
Kimberly, WI 54136
(414) 731-5451

Greater Milwaukee Coin & Jewelry Exchange
4040 N. Calhoun Road
Brookfield, WI 53005
(414) 781-4200

Shorewood Coin Shop
4495 N. Oakland Ave.
Milwaukee, WI 53211
(414) 961-0999

Show Promoters

ANA
818 Cascade Ave.
Colorado Springs, CO
80903

Krause Publications
700 E. State Street
Iola, WI 54990

Kevin Foley
Box 589
Milwaukee, WI 53201

Professional Numismatists Guild, Inc.
3950 Concordia Lane
Fallbrook, CA 92028

Grading Services and Associated Businesses

NGC
Box 1812
Parsippany, NJ 07054-7812
(800)-PROOF67

PCGS
Box 9458
Newport Beach, CA 92658
(800) 447-8848

Capital Collectors Plastics
Box 543IE
Massillon, Ohio 44648-0543

United States Mint
Box 41998
Philadelphia, PA 19101.

To Do List

- WRITE FOR FREE LITERATURE.

Coin World
Box 150,
Sidney OH 45365.

Numismatic News and *Coins*
Krause Publications
700 East State Street
Iola, WI 54990.

COINage
2660 East Main Street
Ventura, CA 93003.

American Numismatic Associaiton
818 Cascade Ave.
Colorado Springs, CO
80903

Professional Numisma-tists Guild (PNG)
Box 430
Van Nuys, CA 91408
(for dealer directory)

Bowers and Merena Galleries
Box 1224
Wolfeboro, NH 03894
(800) 458-4646
fax (603) 569-5319

Stacks
123 West 57th Street
New York, NY 10019
(212) 582-5955
fax (212) 582-1946.

- PREPARE A (PRAC-TICE) WANT LIST.

- ATTEND A COIN SHOW.

- GO TO AN AUCTION.
  register,
  examine coins,
  attend floor session.

- VISIT A COIN SHOP.

- ORDER SOMETHING BY MAIL.

INSTANT EXPERT QUIZ

1. Were United States coins first struck in 1652, 1776, 1787, 1793, or 1861?

2. What is the smallest United States silver coin?

3. What 1933 coin cannot now be legally owned?

4. What kinds of coins were struck at Dahlonega, Georgia?

5. What is a trime?

6. What is an obverse?

7. In 1976 we had a commemorative quarter for the bicentennial celebration. What other commemorative quarters has the United States had?

8. What is a bottom feeder?

9. How can you rip a coin?

10. What was the first one cent coin struck at a branch mint?

11. What is the name of the largest numismatic association in America?

12. What is juice?

13. What is the minimum number of coins necessary to have $2.72, $3.23?

14. What is the connection between the Los Angeles Lakers and numismatics?

15. How much do you have if you have an eagle and a quarter eagle?

16. Name a coin that can be found in circulation with a value significantly higher than face.

17. What is a proof coin?

18. What is a "5"?

19. What usually happens to the price of modern commemoratives after the issue period ends?

20. What is a fresh coin? A slider?

21. What two mints used the D mint mark?

Answers

1. 1793

2. trime (silver 3¢)

3. $20 gold

4. gold coins only

5. 3¢ silver

6. the "front" or side with the main designs

7. 1893 Isabella 25¢

8. someone who only looks for the cheapest prices

9. you can rip a coin by have better knowledge than the seller

10. 1908 San Francisco Indian cent

11. American Numismatic Association (ANA)

12. commission paid by the buyer at an auction

13. three coins each ($2.72: $2.50 + 20¢ + 2¢, $3.23: $3.00 + 20¢ + 3¢)

14. owner of the Lakers (Jerry Buss) is a collector

15. $12.50

16. 1995 double-die 1¢, 1982 10¢, and 1989 25¢ without mint mark

17. a proof is a specially prepared coin of the highest quality; today proofs are for collectors

18. "5" is slang for a coin that grades MS-65

19. prices crash

20. a fresh coin is one that has not appeared on the market recently, a slider is a coin that passes for one in higher condition

21. Dahlonega and Denver

APPENDIX

GLOSSARY

alloy: a mixture of two or more metals.

assay: to analyze and determine the purity of metal.

bag mark: a mark on a coin from contact with other coins in a mint bag.

bullion: gold or silver in the form of bars, plates, etc., but not coins.

business strike: a coin intended for circulation (as opposed to a proof coin specially made for collectors).

bust: a portrait on a coin, usually including the head, neck, and upper shoulders.

clad coinage: coins with a core and outer layer of differing substance. U.S. dimes, quarters, half dollars, and dollars have been clad since 1965.

collar: a metal piece that restrains the expanding metal of a planchet during striking.

commemorative: a coin of special design, issued to honor an outstanding person, place, or event in history.

condition: the physical state of a coin.

counterfeit: a coin or piece of currency imitating a genuine article and intended to deceive buyers or users.

currency: any medium of exchange including coins, paper money, and other items of value used in daily commerce.

denomination: the value represented by specific currency, such as a nickel, dime or dollar.

designer: the artist who creates a coin's design (but does not necessarily engrave the design into a coinage die).

device: a symbol or figure on a coin.

die: a piece of metal bearing the design of the coin. Two dies (obverse and reverse) come together against a coin blank to strike a finished coin.

edge: the outer border of a coin, considered the "third side" of a coin (not to be confused with "rim"). Some coins feature lettering, reeding, or ornamental designs on their edges.

engraver: the person who cuts the design into a coinage die (not necessarily the designer).

error: a coin improperly produced.

face value: the sum for which a coin can be spent or exchanged as opposed to its collector or precious metal value.

field: the portion of a coin's surface not used for design or inscription.

grade: the condition or amount of wear that a coin has received. The numerical scale measures, or grades, coins from About Good-3 to Uncirculated-70.

hairlines: minute lines or scratches on coins usually caused by cleaning or polishing.

incuse: the design of a coin that has been impressed below the coin's surface, rather than the more normal "raised" design protruding above the surface.

inscription: the legend or lettering on a coin.

intrinsic value (melt value): the value of the metal in a coin.

key date: a scarce date required to complete a collection, usually more difficult to find and afford.

legal tender: a coin, note, or other article issued by a government as official money that must be accepted in commerce. Legal tender of coins may be limited to a set amount per transaction.

legend: principal lettering on a coin.

medal: an object usually resembling a coin, but with no monetary status.

mint: a plant that produces coins. Today there are U.S. mints in Philadelphia, Denver, San Francisco, and West Point. Sometimes the government has minted coins at facilities that it called "assay office" or something other than "mint."

mint luster: the dull, frosty, or satiny shine found on uncirculated coins, resulting from the centrifugal flow of metal as dies strike the coin blank.

mint mark: a small letter on a coin identifying which mint struck the coin.

mint set: a complete set of coins of each denomination produced by a particular mint.

mint state: without rub, friction, or wear from circulation.

mintage: the quantity of coins produced.

motto: a phrase or slogan on a coin expressing a principle or ideal.

mule: a coin struck with two dies not meant to be used together.

NCLT: non-circulating legal tender. Coins issued by governments that do not actually circulate. Usually the coins are silver or gold and the face value is well above the bullion value. Such coins are also generally sold to the public at prices well above the face value. United States commemoratives are NCLT.

numismatics: the study and collecting of medals, coins, and articles used as money.

obsolete: a coin design or type that is no longer produced.

obverse: the side of a coin that usually features the date and the principal design.

off-center: a coin that has received an off-center strike from the coin press and has portions of its designs missing.

overstrike: A new coin produced with a previously struck coin used as the planchet.

pattern: an experimental or trial piece, generally of a new design or metal.

planchet: the blank piece of metal on which a coin design is stamped.

proof: a specially produced coin made from highly polished planchets and dies, and often struck twice to accent the design.

proof set: a complete set of proof coins of each denomination made in a year.

relief: any part of a coin's design that is raised above the coin's surface is said to be in relief. The opposite of relief is incuse.

restrike: a coin minted after the year of its date from the original dies.

reverse: the side ("tails") of a coin, usually carrying a design of lesser importance than the obverse.

rim: the raised circumference of a coin's obverse and reverse, circling the design and protecting it from wear.

roll: coins packaged by banks or dealers in the following quantities: 50 cents, 40 nickels, 50 dimes, 40 quarters, 20 half dollars, 20 dollars.

series: all dates and mint marks of a specific design and denomination such as the Mercury dime series or Buffalo nickel series.

strike: the process of stamping a coin blank with a die bearing the design. A strike may be considered full, average, or weak on a particular coin, and will affect the value of rare coins.

toning: coloring caused by chemical reaction to the air or other materials over time.

type collecting: assembling coins on the basis of design instead of by date and mint mark; collecting a coin of each different design in a series.

uncirculated: without rub, friction or wear from circulation.

variety: A minor change from the basic design type of a coin.

year set: collection including each year of issue of a certain type of coin, though not necessarily including each mint issue.

BIBLIOGRAPHY

Hundreds of books have been published on United States numismatics. The following books been useful in writing this *Instant Expert* guide and are highly recommended.

ALEXANDER, DAVID T., editor. *Coin World Comprehensive Catalog & Encyclopedia of United States Coins.* New York: World Almanac, 1991.

BOWERS, Q. DAVID. *Commemorative Coins of the United States: a Complete Encyclopedia,* Bowers and Merena Galleries, Wolfeboro, NH, 1991.

BREEN, WALTER. *Walter Breen's Complete Encyclopedia of U.S. and Colonial Coins.* New York: Doubleday, 1988.

SCHWAN, CARLTON F., AND JOSEPH E. BOLING. *World War II Remembered.* Port Clinton, Ohio: BNR Press, 1995.

SWIATEK, ANTHONY, AND WALTER BREEN. *The Encyclopedia of United States and Silver and Gold Commemorative Coins 1892-1954.* Arco Publications, NY, 1981.

TRAVERS, SCOTT A. *The Coin Collector's Survival Manual.* Chicago: Bonus Books, 1994.

YEOMAN, R. S., AND KENNETH BRESSETT, editor. *A Guide Book of United States Coins.* Racine, Wis.: Western Publishing Company, 1995.

QUICK REFERENCE COIN TYPES

Half Cents 1793-1857
liberty cap 1793–1797
draped bust 1800–1808
classic head 1809–1836
coronet 1840–1857

Large Cents 1793-1857
flowing hair 1793
Liberty cap 1793–1795
draped bust 1796–1807
classic head 1808–1814
coronet 1816-1857

Small Cents 1856-present
flying eagle 1856–1858
Indian head 1859–1909
Lincoln 1909–present

Two Cents 1864–1873
Three Cents (silver)
1851–1873
Three Cents (nickel)
1865–1889

Five Cents 1866-present
shield 1866–1883
Liberty head 1883–1912
Indian head or buffalo
    1913–1938
Jefferson 1938–present

Half Dimes 1794–1873
flowing hair 1794–1795
draped bust 1796–1805
capped bust 1829–1837
Liberty seated 1837–1873

Dimes 1796–present
draped bust 1796–1807
capped bust 1809–1837
Liberty seated 1837–1891
Barber or Liberty head
    1892–1916
Winged Liberty head or
    Mercury 1916–1945
Roosevelt 1946–present

Twenty Cents 1875–1878
Liberty seated

Quarters 1796–present
draped bust type 1796–1807
capped bust 1815–1818
Liberty seated 1838–1891
Barber or Liberty head
    1892–1916
standing Liberty 1916–1930
Washington 1932–present

Half Dollars 1794–present
flowing hair 1794–1795
draped bust 1796–1807
Liberty seated 1839–1891
Barber or Liberty head
    1892–1915
Liberty walking 1916–1947
Franklin-Liberty Bell
    1948–1963
Kennedy 1964-present

Silver (and clad) Dollars
flowing hair 1794–1795
draped bust 1795–1804
Liberty seated 1840–1873
trade dollar 1873–1885
Morgan 1878–1921
Peace 1921–1935
Eisenhower 1971–1978
Anthony 1979–1981

Gold
one dollar 1849–1889
Liberty head 1849–1854
Indian head 1854–1889

Quarter Eagle ($2.50)
1796-1929
capped bust left and right
    1796–1808
capped head 1821–1824
classic head 1834–1839
coronet 1840–1907
Indian head 1908–1929

Three Dollars 1854–1889
Four Dollars, Stella
    1879–1880

Half Eagles ($5) 1795–1929
capped bust left and right
    1796–1812
capped head 1813–1834
classic head 1834–1838
coronet 1839–1908
Indian head 1908–1929

Eagles ($10) 1795–1933
capped bust left and right
    1795–1804
Liberty 1838–1866
Indian head 1907–1933

Double Eagles $20
    1849–1933
Liberty 1849–1907
Saint-Gaudens 1907–1933

EPILOGUE

THE CROWN JEWELS OF
UNITED STATES NUMISMATICS

The 1804 silver dollar and the 1913 Liberty nickel are rarities of which legends are made. Their lore is so widespread that most noncollectors are at least vaguely aware of these coins. Other coins are actually more rare, but no other coins are as well known or coveted as these two pieces. Their histories are replete with mystery and intrigue that continue to this day.

The 1913 Liberty nickel was made famous by B. Max Mehl who advertised in the 1930s to pay $50 for them. Liberty nickels were still commonly found in circulation so the public eagerly searched for the coin that would bring such a windfall. The catch was that only five such coins existed. People also wrote by the millions to buy Mehl's *Star Rare Coin Encyclopedia* that listed other coins that Mehl would buy at similar princely sums.

It seems that one or more mint employee struck the five coins surreptitiously. The coin made its first appearance in 1919 when an advertisement appeared in the December issue of *The Numismatist*. Samuel W. Brown advertised to buy these coins at $500 each. Later he raised his advertised price to $600, then he exhibited the five pieces at the 1920 convention of the American Numismatic Association. The five pieces were sold to Stephen K. Nagy then to Wayte Raymond, Colonel E. H. R. Green (son of the notorious stingy millionaire "witch of Wall Street" Hetty Green), and finally to Burdette G. Johnson. The coins were then sold by Johnson to different people.

The 1913 Liberty Head nickel and 1804 silver dollar are legendary coins. They are known by the general public and honored by collectors.

The pedigrees of the five single pieces are traced in *Walter Breen's Complete Encyclopedia of U.S. and Colonial Coins*. Two of the five coins are permanently housed in collections (American Numismatic Association and Smithsonian Institution) and another has been "missing" for many years. George O. Walton owned one of the nickels. Since he was killed in an automobile accident, the whereabouts of his piece has not been confirmed. Rumors that his coin was lost to highway rubble during the accident are unfounded, but they add to the lore of the remarkable 1913 Liberty nickel.

Although mint records state that 19,570 silver dollars were struck in 1804, only 15 examples are known in collections! It was common practice at the time to continue using dies at the end of the year so the 20 silver dollars reported for 1804 are actually dated 1803!

The 1804 dollars were not even struck until 1834 and some more were struck in 1859! Basically these coins were created to meet the demands of collectors. An entire book has been written about these wonderful coins: *The Fantastic 1804 Dollar* by Eric P. Newman and Kenneth E. Bressett. It is recommended reading.

Both the 1804 silver dollar and the 1913 Liberty nickel have sold for a million dollars or more each!

INDEX